So quickly did the man appear that Tom was almost
upon him in an instant.

Page 89

Tom Swift and His Motor Cycle.

TOM SWIFT AND HIS MOTOR-CYCLE

OR

FUN AND ADVENTURES ON THE ROAD

BY
VICTOR APPLETON

AUTHOR OF "TOM SWIFT AND HIS MOTOR-BOAT," "TOM SWIFT AND HIS AIR-SHIP," "TOM SWIFT AND HIS SUBMARINE BOAT," ETC

FACSIMILE EDITION

1992
BEDFORD, MA
APPLEWOOD BOOKS

For further information about these editions, please write: Applewood Books, P.O. Box 365, Bedford, MA 01730.

10 9 8 7 6 5

Library of Congress Cataloging-in-Publication Data
Appleton, Victor, II.
    Tom Swift and his motor-cycle, or, Fun and adventures on the road / by Victor Appleton. —Facsimile ed.
            p.   cm.
    Summary: Having longed for a motorcycle, bright ingenious Tom Swift gets one unexpectedly.
    ISBN 1-55709-175-7
    [1. Motorcycles—Fiction. 2. Adventure and adventurers—Fiction.] I. Title. II. Title: fun and adventures on the road.
PZ7.A653Moc   1992
[Fic]—dc20   92-28649
                                                      CIP
                                                      AC

TOM SWIFT AND HIS MOTOR-CYCLE

OR

FUN AND ADVENTURES ON THE ROAD

BY

VICTOR APPLETON

AUTHOR OF "TOM SWIFT AND HIS MOTOR-BOAT," "TOM SWIFT AND HIS AIR-SHIP," "TOM SWIFT AND HIS SUBMARINE BOAT," ETC

NEW YORK
GROSSET & DUNLAP
PUBLISHERS
Made in the United States of America

CONTENTS

CONTENTS

TOM SWIFT AND HIS MOTOR-CYCLE

CHAPTER I

A NARROW ESCAPE

"THAT's the way to do it! Whoop her up, Andy! Shove the spark lever over, and turn on more gasolene! We'll make a record this trip."

Two lads in the tonneau of a touring car, that was whirling along a country road, leaned forward to speak to the one at the steering wheel. The latter was a red-haired youth, with somewhat squinty eyes, and not a very pleasant face, but his companions seemed to regard him with much favor. Perhaps it was because they were riding in his automobile.

"Whoop her up, Andy!" added the lad on the seat beside the driver. "This is immense!"

"I rather thought you'd like it," remarked Andy Foger, as he turned the car to avoid a stone in the road. "I'll make things hum around Shopton!"

"You have made them hum already, Andy," commented the lad beside him. "My ears are ringing. Wow! There goes my cap!"

As the boy spoke, the breeze, created by the speed at which the car was traveling, lifted off his cap, and sent it whirling to the rear.

Andy Foger turned for an instant's glance behind. Then he opened the throttle still wider, and exclaimed:

"Let it go, Sam. We can get another. I want to see what time I can make to Mansburg! I want to break a record, if I can."

"Look out, or you'll break something else!" cried a lad on the rear seat. "There's a fellow on a bicycle just ahead of us. Take care, Andy!"

"Let him look out for himself," retorted Foger, as he bent lower over the steering wheel, for the car was now going at a terrific rate. The youth on the bicycle was riding slowly along, and did not see the approaching automobile until it was nearly upon him. Then, with a mean grin, Andy Foger pressed the rubber bulb of the horn with sudden energy, sending out a series of alarming blasts.

"It's Tom Swift!" cried Sam Snedecker. "Look out, or you'll run him down!"

"Let him keep out of my way," retorted Andy savagely.

The youth on the wheel, with a sudden spurt of speed, tried to cross the highway. He did manage to do it, but by such a narrow margin that in very terror Andy Foger shut off the power, jammed down the brakes and steered to one side. So suddenly was he obliged to swerve over that the ponderous machine skidded and went into the ditch at the side of the road, where it brought up, tilting to one side.

Tom Swift, his face rather pale from his narrow escape, leaped from his bicycle, and stood regarding the automobile. As for the occupants of that machine, from Andy Foger, the owner, to the three cronies who were riding with him, they all looked very much astonished.

"Are we—is it damaged any, Andy?" asked Sam Snedecker.

"I hope not," growled Andy. "If my car's hurt it's Tom Swift's fault!"

He leaped from his seat and made a hurried inspection of the machine. He found nothing the matter, though it was more from good luck than good management. Then Andy turned and looked savagely at Tom Swift. The latter, standing his wheel up against the fence, walked forward.

"What do you mean by getting in the way like that?" demanded Andy with a scowl. "Don't you see that you nearly upset me?"

"Well, I like your nerve, Andy Foger!" cried Tom. "What do you mean by nearly running me down? Why didn't you sound your horn? You automobilists take too much for granted! You were going faster than the legal rate, anyhow!"

"I was, eh?" sneered Andy.

"Yes, you were, and you know it. I'm the one to make a kick, not you. You came pretty near hitting me. Me getting in your way! I guess I've got some rights on the road!"

"Aw, go on!" growled Andy, for he could think of nothing else to say. "Bicycles are a back number, anyhow."

"It isn't so very long ago that you had one," retorted Tom. "First you fellows know, you'll be pulled in for speeding."

"I guess we had better go slower, Andy," advised Sam in a low voice. "I don't want to be arrested."

"Leave this to me," retorted Andy. "I'm running this tour. The next time you get in my way I'll run you down!" he threatened Tom. "Come on, fellows, we're late now, and can't make a record run, all on account of him," and Andy got back into the car, followed by his cronies, who had hurriedly alighted after their thrilling stop.

"If you try anything like this again you'll wish you hadn't," declared Tom, and he watched the automobile party ride off.

"Oh, forget it!" snapped back Andy, and he laughed, his companions joining.

Tom Swift said nothing in reply. Slowly he remounted his wheel and rode off, but his thoughts toward Andy Foger were not very pleasant ones. Andy was the son of a wealthy man of the town, and his good fortune in the matter of money seemed to have spoiled him, for he was a bully and a coward. Several times he and Tom Swift had clashed, for Andy was overbearing. But this was the first time Andy had shown such a vindictive spirit.

"He thinks he can run over everything since he got his new auto," commented Tom aloud as he rode on. "He'll have a smash-up some day, if he isn't careful. He's too fond of speeding. I wonder where he and his crowd are going?"

Musing over his narrow escape Tom rode on, and was soon at his home, where he lived with his widowed father, Barton Swift, a wealthy inventor, and the latter's housekeeper, Mrs. Baggert. Approaching a machine shop, one of several built near his house by Mr. Swift, in which he conducted experiments and constructed apparatus, Tom was met by his parent.

"What's the matter, Tom?" asked Mr. Swift. "You look as if something had happened."

"Something very nearly did," answered the youth, and related his experience on the road.

"Humph," remarked the inventor; "your little pleasure-jaunt might have ended disastrously. I suppose Andy and his chums are off on their trip. I remember Mr. Foger speaking to me about it the other day. He said Andy and some companions were going on a tour, to be gone a week or more. Well, I'm glad it was no worse. But have you anything special to do, Tom?"

"No; I was just riding for pleasure, and if you want me to do anything, I'm ready."

"Then I wish you'd take this letter to Mansburg for me. I want it registered, and I don't wish to mail it in the Shopton post-office. It's too important, for it's about a valuable invention."

"The new turbine motor, dad?"

"That's it. And on your way I wish you'd stop in Merton's machine shop and get some bolts he's making for me."

"I will. Is that the letter?" and Tom extended his hand for a missive his father held.

"Yes. Please be careful of it. It's to my lawyers in Washington regarding the final steps in getting a patent for the turbine. That's why I'm so particular about not wanting it mailed here. Several times before I have posted letters here, only to have the information contained in them leak out before my attorneys received them. I do not want that to happen in this case. Another thing; don't speak about my new invention in Merton's shop when you stop for the bolts."

"Why, do you think he gave out information concerning your work?"

"Well, not exactly. He might not mean to, but he told me the other day that some strangers were making inquiries of him, about whether he ever did any work for me."

"What did he tell them?"

"He said that he occasionally did, but that most of my inventive work was done in my own shops, here. He wanted to know why the men were asking such questions, and one of them said they expected to open a machine shop soon, and wanted to ascertain if they might figure on getting any of my trade. But I don't believe that was their object."

"What do you think it was?"

"I don't know, exactly, but I was somewhat alarmed when I heard this from Merton. So I am going to take no risks. That's why I send this letter to Mansburg. Don't lose it, and don't forget about the bolts. Here is a blue-print of them, so you can see if they come up to the specifications."

Tom rode off on his wheel, and was soon spinning down the road.

"I wonder if I'll meet Andy Foger and his cronies again?" he thought. "Not very likely to, I guess, if they're off on a tour. Well, I'm just as well satisfied. He and I always seem to get into trouble when we meet." Tom was not destined to meet Andy again that day, but the time was to come when the red-haired bully was to cause Tom Swift no little trouble, and get him into danger besides. So Tom rode along, thinking over what his father had said to him about the letter he carried.

Mr. Barton Swift was a natural inventor. From a boy he had been interested in things mechanical, and one of his first efforts had been to arrange a system of pulleys, belts and gears so that the windmill would operate the churn in the old farmhouse where he was born. The fact that the mill went so fast that it broke the churn all to pieces did not discourage him, and he at once set to work changing the gears. His father had to buy a new churn, but the young inventor made his plan work on the second trial, and thereafter his mother found butter-making easy.

From then on Barton Swift lived in a world of inventions. People used to say he would never amount to anything, that inventors never did, but Mr. Swift proved them all wrong by amassing a considerable fortune out of his many patents. He grew up, married and had one son, Tom. Mrs. Barton died when Tom was three years old, and since then he had lived with his father and a succession of nurses and housekeepers. The last woman to have charge of the household was a Mrs. Baggert, a motherly widow, and she succeeded so well, and Tom and his father formed such an attachment for her, that she was regarded as a fixture, and had now been in charge ten years.

Mr. Swift and his son lived in a handsome house on the outskirts of the village of Shopton, in New York State. The village was near a large body of water, which I shall call Lake Carlopa, and there Tom and his father used to spend many pleasant days boating, for Tom and the inventor were better chums than many boys are, and they were often seen together in a craft rowing about, or fishing. Of course Tom had some boy friends, but he went with his father more often than he did with them.

Though many of Mr. Swift's inventions paid him well, he was constantly seeking to perfect others. To this end he had built near his home several machine shops, with engines, lathes and apparatus for various kinds of work. Tom, too, had the inventive fever in his veins, and had planned some useful implements and small ma-chines.

Along the pleasant country roads on a fine day in April rode Tom Swift on his way to Mansburg to register the letter. As he descended a little hill he saw, some distance away, but coming to-ward him, a great cloud of dust.

"Somebody must be driving a herd of cattle along the road," thought Tom. "I hope they don't get in my way, or, rather, I hope I don't get in theirs. Guess I'd better keep to one side, yet there isn't any too much room."

The dust-cloud came nearer. It was so dense that whoever or whatever was making it could not be distinguished.

"Must be a lot of cattle in that bunch," mused the young inventor, "but I shouldn't think they'd trot them so on a warm day like this. Maybe they're stampeded. If they are I've got to look out." This idea caused him some alarm.

He tried to peer through the dust-cloud, but could not. Nearer and nearer it came. Tom kept on, taking care to get as far to the side of the road as he could. Then from the midst of the enveloping mass came the sound of a steady "chug-chug."

"It's a motor-cycle!" exclaimed Tom. "He must have his muffler wide open, and that's kicking up as much dust as the wheels do. Whew! But whoever's on it will look like a clay image at the end of the line!"

Now that he knew it was a fellow-cyclist who was raising such a disturbance, Tom turned more toward the middle of the road. As yet he had not had a sight of the rider, but the explosions of the motor were louder. Suddenly, when the first advancing particles of dust reached him, almost making him sneeze, Tom caught sight of the rider. He was a man of middle age, and he was clinging to the handle-bars of the machine. The motor was going at full speed.

Tom quickly turned to one side, to avoid the worst of the dust. The motor-cyclist glanced at the youth, but this act nearly proved disastrous for him. He took his eyes from the road ahead for just a moment, and he did not see a large stone directly in his path. His front wheel hit it, and the heavy machine, which he could not control very well, skidded over toward the lad on the bicycle. The motor-cyclist bounced up in the air from the saddle, and nearly lost his hold on the handle-bars.

"Look out!" cried Tom. "You'll smash into me!"

"I'm—I'm—try — ing — not — to!" were the words that were rattled out of the middle-aged man.

Tom gave his wheel a desperate twist to get out of the way. The motor-cyclist tried to do the same, but the machine he was on appeared to want matters its own way. He came straight for Tom, and a disastrous collision might have resulted had not another stone been in the way. The front wheel hit this, and was swerved to one side. The motor-cycle flashed past Tom, just grazing his wheel, and then was lost to sight beyond in a cloud of dust that seemed to follow it like a halo.

"Why don't you learn to ride before you come out on the road!" cried Tom somewhat angrily.

Like an echo from the dust-cloud came floating back these words:

"I'm—try—ing—to!" Then the sound of the explosions became fainter.

"Well, he's got lots to learn yet!" exclaimed Tom. "That's twice to-day I've nearly been run down. I expect I'd better look out for the third time. They say that's always fatal," and the lad leaped from his wheel. "Wonder if he bent any of my spokes?" the young inventor continued as he inspected his bicycle.

CHAPTER II

"EVERYTHING seems to be all right," Tom re-marked, "but another inch or so and he'd have crashed into me. I wonder who he was? I wish I had a machine like that. I could make better time than I can on my bicycle. Perhaps I'll get one some day. Well, I might as well ride on."

Tom was soon at Mansburg, and going to the post-office handed in the letter for registry. Bearing in mind his father's words, he looked about to see if there were any suspicious characters, but the only person he noticed was a well-dressed man, with a black mustache, who seemed to be intently studying the schedule of the arrival and departure of the mails.

"Do you want the receipt for the registered letter sent to you here or at Shopton?" asked the clerk of Tom. "Come to think of it, though, it will have to come here, and you can call for it. I'll have it returned to Mr. Barton Swift, care of

13

general delivery, and you can get it the next time you are over," for the clerk knew Tom.

"That will do," answered our hero, and as he turned away from the window he saw that the man who had been inquiring about the mails was regarding him curiously. Tom thought nothing of it at the time, but there came an occasion when he wished that he had taken more careful note of the well-dressed individual. As the youth passed out of the outer door he saw the man walk over to the registry window.

"He seems to have considerable mail business," thought Tom, and then the matter passed from his mind as he mounted his wheel and hurried to the machine shop.

"Say, I'm awfully sorry," announced Mr. Merton when Tom said he had come for the bolts, "but they're not quite done. They need polishing. I know I promised them to your father to-day, and he can have them, but he was very particular about the polish, and as one of my best workers was taken sick, I'm a little behind."

"How long will it take to polish them?" asked Tom.

"Oh, about an hour. In fact, a man is working on them now. If you could call this afternoon they'll be ready. Can you?"

"I s'pose I've got to," replied Tom good-naturedly. "Guess I'll have to stay in Mansburg for dinner. I can't get back to Shopton in time now."

"I'll be sure to have them for you after dinner," promised Mr. Merton. "Now, there's a matter I want to speak to you about, Tom. Has your father any idea of giving the work he has been turning over to me to some other firm?"

"Not that I know of. Why?" and the lad showed his wonder.

"Well, I'll tell you why. Some time ago there was a stranger in here, asking about your father's work. I told Mr. Swift of it at the time. The stranger said then that he and some others were thinking of opening a machine shop, and he wanted to find out whether they would be likely to get any jobs from your father. I told the man I knew nothing about Mr. Swift's business, and he went away. I didn't hear any more of it, though of course I didn't want to lose your father's trade. Now a funny thing happened. Only this morning the same man was back here, and he was making particular inquiries about your father's private machine shops."

"He was?" exclaimed Tom excitedly.

"Yes. He wanted to know where they were located, how they were laid out, and what sort of work he did in them."

"What did you tell him?"

"Nothing at all. I suspected something, and I said the best way for him to find out would be to go and see your father. Wasn't that right?"

"Sure. Dad doesn't want his business known any more than he can help. What do you suppose they wanted?"

"Well, the man talked as though he and his partners would like to buy your father's shops."

"I don't believe he'd sell. He has them arranged just for his own use in making patents, and I'm sure he would not dispose of them."

"Well, that's what I thought, but I didn't tell the man so. I judged it would be best for him to find out for himself."

"What was the man's name?"

"He didn't tell me, and I didn't ask him."

"How did he look?"

"Well, he was well dressed, wore kid gloves and all that, and he had a little black mustache."

Tom started, and Mr. Merton noticed it.

"Do you know him?" he asked.

"No," replied Tom, "but I saw——" Then he stopped. He recalled the man he had seen in the post-office. He answered this description, but it was too vague to be certain.

"Did you say you'd seen him?" asked Mr. Merton, regarding Tom curiously.

"No—yes—that is—well, I'll tell my father about it," stammered Tom, who concluded that it would be best to say nothing of his suspicions. "I'll be back right after dinner, Mr. Merton. Please have the bolts ready for me, if you can."

"I will. Is your father going to use them in a new machine?"

"Yes; dad is always making new machines," answered the youth, as the most polite way of not giving the proprietor of the shop any information. "I'll be back right after dinner," he called as he went out to get on his wheel.

Tom was much puzzled. He felt certain that the man in the post-office and the one who had questioned Mr. Merton were the same.

"There is something going on, that dad should know about," reflected Tom. "I must tell him. I don't believe it will be wise to send any more of his patent work over to Merton. We must do it in the shops at home, and dad and I will have to keep our eyes open. There may be spies about seeking to discover something about his new turbine motor. I'll hurry back with those bolts and tell dad. But first I must get lunch. I'll go to the restaurant and have a good feed while I'm at it."

Tom had plenty of spending money, some of which came from a small patent he had marketed himself. He left his wheel outside the restaurant, first taking the precaution to chain the wheels, and then went inside. Tom was hungry and ordered a good meal. He was about half way through it when some one called his name.

"Hello, Ned!" he answered, looking up to see a youth about his own age. "Where did you blow in from?"

"Oh, I came over from Shopton this morning," replied Ned Newton, taking a seat at the table with Tom. The two lads were chums, and in their younger days had often gone fishing, swimming and hunting together. Now Ned worked in the Shopton bank, and Tom was so busy helping his father, so they did not see each other so often.

"On business or pleasure?" asked Tom, putting some more sugar in his coffee.

"Business. I had to bring some papers over from our bank to the First National here. But what about you?"

"Oh, I came on dad's account."

"Invented anything new?" asked Ned as he gave his order to the waitress.

"No, nothing since the egg-beater I was telling you about. But I'm working on some things."

"Why don't you invent an automobile or an airship?"

"Maybe I will some day, but, speaking of autos, did you see the one Andy Foger has?"

"Yes; it's a beaut! Have you seen it?"

"Altogether at too close range. He nearly ran over me this morning," and the young inventor related the occurrence.

"Oh, Andy always was too fresh," commented Ned; "and since his father let him get the touring car I suppose he'll be worse than ever."

"Well, if he tries to run me down again he'll get into trouble," declared Tom, calling for a second cup of coffee.

The two chums began conversing on more congenial topics, and Ned was telling of a new camera he had, when, from a table directly behind him, Tom heard some one say in rather loud tones:

"The plant is located in Shopton, all right, and the buildings are near Swift's house."

Tom started, and listened more intently.

"That will make it more difficult," one man answered. "But if the invention is as valuable as——"

"Hush!" came a caution from another of the party. "This is too public a place to discuss the matter. Wait until we get out. One of us will have to see Swift, of course, and if he proves stubborn——"

"I guess you'd better hush yourself," retorted the man who had first spoken, and then the voices subsided.

But Tom Swift had overheard something which made him vaguely afraid. He started so at the sound of his father's name that he knocked a fork from the table.

"What's the matter; getting nervous?" asked Ned with a laugh.

"I guess so," replied Tom, and when he stooped to pick the fork up, not waiting for the girl who was serving at his table, he stole a look at the strangers who had just entered. He was startled to note that one of the men was the same he had seen in the post-office—the man who answered the description of the one who had been inquiring of Mr. Merton about the Swift shops.

"I'm going to keep my ears open," thought Tom as he went on eating his dinner.

CHAPTER III

IN A SMASH-UP

THOUGH the young inventor listened intently, in an endeavor to hear the conversation of the men at the table behind him, all he could catch was an indistinct murmur. The strangers appeared to have heeded the caution of one of their number and were speaking in low tones.

Tom and Ned finished their meal, and started to leave the restaurant. As Mr. Swift's son passed the table where the men sat they looked up quickly at him. Two of them gave Tom but a passing glance, but one—he whom the young inventor had noticed in the post-office—stared long and intently.

"I think he will know me the next time he sees me," thought Tom, and he boldly returned the glance of the stranger.

The bolts were ready when the inventor's son called at the machine shop a second time, and making a package of them Tom fastened it to the saddle of his bicycle. He started for home at a fast pace, and was just turning from a cross road into the main highway when he saw ahead of him a woman driving a light wagon. As the sun flashed on Tom's shining wheel the horse gave a sudden leap, swerved to one side, and then bolted down the dusty stretch, the woman screaming at the top of her voice.

"A runaway!" cried Tom; "and partly my fault, too!"

Waiting not an instant the lad bent over his handle-bars and pedaled with all his force. His bicycle seemed fairly to leap forward after the galloping horse.

"Sit still! Don't jump out! Don't jump!" yelled the young inventor. "I'll try to catch him!" for the woman was standing up in front of the seat and leaning forward, as if about to leap from the wagon.

"She's lost her head," thought Tom. "No wonder! That's a skittish horse."

Faster and faster he rode, bending all his energies to overtake the animal. The wagon was swaying from side to side, and more than once the woman just saved herself from being thrown out by grasping the edge of the seat. She found that her standing position was a dangerous one and crouched on the bottom of the swaying vehicle.

"That's better!" shouted Tom, but it is doubtful if she heard him, for the rattling of the wagon and the hoofbeats of the horse drowned all other sounds. "Sit still!" he shouted. "I'll stop the horse for you!"

Trying to imagine himself in a desperate race, in order to excite himself to greater speed, Tom continued on. He was now even with the tail-board of the wagon, and slowly creeping up. The woman was all huddled up in a lump.

"Grab the reins! Grab the reins!" shouted Tom. "Saw on the bit! That will stop him!"

The occupant of the wagon turned to look at the lad. Tom saw that she was a handsome young lady. "Grab the reins!" he cried again. "Pull hard!"

"I—I can't!" she answered frightenedly. "They have dropped down! Oh, do please stop the horse! I'm so—so frightened!"

"I'll stop him!" declared the youth firmly, and he set his teeth hard. Then he saw the reason the fair driver could not grasp the lines. They had slipped over the dashboard and were trailing on the ground.

The horse was slacking speed a bit now, for the pace was telling on his wind. Tom saw his opportunity, and with a sudden burst of energy was at the animal's head. Steering his wheel with one hand, with the other the lad made a grab for the reins near the bit. The horse swerved frightenedly to one side, but Tom swung in the same direction. He grasped the leather and then, with a kick, he freed himself from the bicycle, giving it a shove to one side. He was now clinging to the reins with both hands, and, being a muscular lad and no lightweight, his bulk told.

"Sit—still!" panted our hero to the young woman, who had arisen to the seat. "I'll have him stopped in half a minute now!"

It was in less time than that, for the horse, finding it impossible to shake off the grip of Tom, began to slow from a gallop to a trot, then to a canter, and finally to a slow walk. A moment later the horse had stopped, breathing heavily from his run.

"There, there, now!" spoke Tom soothingly. "You're all right, old fellow. I hope you're not hurt"— this to the young lady—and Tom made a motion to raise his cap, only to find that it had blown off.

"Oh, no—no; I'm more frightened than hurt."

"It was all my fault," declared the young inventor. "I should not have swung into the road so suddenly. My bicycle alarmed your horse."

"Oh, I fancy Dobbin is easily disturbed," admitted the fair driver. "I can't thank you enough for stopping him. You saved me from a bad accident."

"It was the least I could do. Are you all right now?" and he handed up the dangling reins. "I think Dobbin, as you call him, has had enough of running," went on Tom, for the horse was now quiet.

"I hope so. Yes, I am all right. I trust your wheel is not damaged. If it is, my father, Mr. Amos Nestor, of Mansburg, will gladly pay for its repair."

This reminded the young inventor of his bicycle, and making sure that the horse would not start up again, he went to where his wheel and his cap lay. He found that the only damage to the bicycle was a few bent spokes, and, straightening them and having again apologized to the young woman, receiving in turn her pardon and thanks, and learning that her name was Mary Nestor, Tom once more resumed his trip. The wagon followed him at a distance, the horse evincing no desire now to get out of a slow amble.

"Well, things are certainly happening to me to-day," mused Tom as he pedaled on. "That might have been a serious runaway if there'd been anything in the road."

Tom did not stop to think that he had been mainly instrumental in preventing a bad accident, as he had been the innocent cause of starting the runaway, but Tom was ever a modest lad. His arms were wrenched from jerking on the bridle, but he did not mind that much, and bent over the handle-bars to make up for lost time.

Our hero was within a short distance of his house and was coasting easily along when, just ahead of him, he saw a cloud of dust, very similar to the one that had, some time before, concealed the inexperienced motor-cyclist.

"I wonder if that's him again?" thought Tom. "If it is I'm going to hang back until I see which way he's headed. No use running any more risks."

Almost at that moment a puff of wind blew some of the dust to one side. Tom had a glimpse of the man on the puffing machine.

"It's the same chap!" he exclaimed aloud; "and he's going the same way I am. Well, I'll not try to catch up to him. I wonder what he's been doing all this while, that he hasn't gotten any farther than this? Either he's been riding back and forth, or else he's been resting. My, but he certainly is scooting along!"

The wind carried to Tom the sound of the explosions of the motor, and he could see the man clinging tightly to the handle-bars. The rider was almost in front of Tom's house now, when, with a suddenness that caused the lad to utter an exclamation of alarm, the stranger turned his machine right toward a big oak tree.

"What's he up to?" cried Tom excitedly. "Does he think he can climb that, or is he giving an exhibition by showing how close he can come and not hit it?"

A moment later the motor-cyclist struck the tree a glancing blow. The man went flying over the handle-bars, the machine was shunted to the ditch along the road, and falling over on one side the motor raced furiously. The rider lay in a heap at the foot of the tree.

"My, that was a smash!" cried Tom. "He must be killed!" and bending forward, he raced toward the scene of the accident.

CHAPTER IV

TOM AND A MOTOR-CYCLE

WHEN Tom reached the prostrate figure on the grass at the foot of the old oak tree, the youth bent quickly over the man. There was an ugly cut on his head, and blood was flowing from it. But Tom quickly noticed that the stranger was breathing, though not very strongly.

"Well, he's not dead—just yet!" exclaimed the youth with a sigh of relief. "But I guess he's pretty badly hurt. I must get help—no, I'll take him into our house. It's not far. I'll call dad."

Leaning his wheel against the tree Tom started for his home, about three hundred feet away, and then he noticed that the stranger's motor-cycle was running at full speed on the ground.

"Guess I'd better shut off the power!" he exclaimed. "No use letting the machine be ruined." Tom had a natural love for machinery, and it hurt him almost as much to see a piece of fine apparatus abused as it did to see an animal mistreated. It was the work of a moment to shut off the gasolene and spark, and then the youth raced on toward his house.

"Where's dad?" he called to Mrs. Baggert, who was washing the dishes.

"Out in one of the shops," replied the housekeeper. "Why, Tom" she went on hurriedly as she saw how excited he was, "whatever has happened?"

"Man hurt—out in front—motor-cycle smash— I'm going to bring him in here—get some things ready—I'll find dad!"

"Bless and save us!" cried Mrs. Baggert. "Whatever are we coming to? Who's hurt? How did it happen? Is he dead?"

"Haven't time to talk now!" answered Tom, rushing from the house. "Dad and I will bring him in here."

Tom found his father in one of the three small machine shops on the grounds about the Swift home. The youth hurriedly told what had happened.

"Of course we'll bring him right in here!" assented Mr. Swift, putting aside the work upon which he was engaged. "Did you tell Mrs. Baggert?"

"Yes, and she's all excited."

"Well, she can't help it, being a woman, I suppose. But we'll manage. Do you know the man?"

"Never saw him before to-day, when he tried to run me down. Guess he doesn't know much about motor-cycles. But come on, dad. He may bleed to death."

Father and son hurried to where the stranger lay. As they bent over him he opened his eyes and asked faintly:

"Where am I? What happened?"

"You're all right—in good hands," said Mr. Swift. "Are you much hurt?"

"Not much—mostly stunned, I guess. What happened?" he repeated.

"You and your motor-cycle tried to climb a tree," remarked Tom with grim humor.

"Oh, yes, I remember now. I couldn't seem to steer out of the way. And I couldn't shut off the power in time. Is the motor-cycle much damaged?"

"The front wheel is," reported Tom, after an inspection, "and there are some other breaks, but I guess——"

"I wish it was all smashed!" exclaimed the man vigorously. "I never want to see it again!"

"Why, don't you like it?" asked Tom eagerly.

"No, and I never will," the man spoke faintly but determinedly.

"Never mind now," interposed Mr. Swift. "Don't excite yourself. My son and I will take you to our house and send for a doctor."

"I'll bring the motor-cycle, after we've carried you in," added Tom.

"Don't worry about the machine. I never want to see it again!" went on the man, rising to a sitting position. "It nearly killed me twice to-day. I'll never ride again."

"You'll feel differently after the doctor fixes you up," said Mr. Swift with a smile.

"Doctor! I don't need a doctor," cried the stranger. "I am only bruised and shaken up."

"You have a bad cut on your head," said Tom.

"It isn't very deep," went on the injured man, placing his fingers on it. "Fortunately I struck the tree a glancing blow. If you will allow me to rest in your house a little while and give me some plaster for the cut I shall be all right again."

"Can you walk, or shall we carry you?" asked Tom's father.

"Oh, I can walk, if you'll support me a little." And the stranger proved that he could do this by getting to his feet and taking a few steps. Mr. Swift and his son took hold of his arms and led him to the house. There he was placed on a lounge and given some simple restoratives by Mrs.

Baggert, who, when she found the accident was not serious, recovered her composure.

"I must have been unconscious for a few minutes," went on the man.

"You were," explained Tom. "When I got up to you I thought you were dead, until I saw you breathe. Then I shut off the power of your machine and ran in for dad. I've got the motor-cycle outside. You can't ride it for some time, I'm afraid, Mr.—er——" and Tom stopped in some confusion, for he realized that he did not know the man's name.

"I beg your pardon for not introducing myself before," went on the stranger. "I'm Wakefield Damon, of Waterfield. But don't worry about me riding that machine again. I never shall."

"Oh, perhaps——" began Mr. Swift.

"No, I never shall," went on Mr. Damon positively. "My doctor told me to get it, as he thought riding around the country would benefit my health. I shall tell him his prescription nearly killed me."

"And me too," added Tom with a laugh.

"How—why—are you the young man I nearly ran down this morning?" asked Mr. Damon, suddenly sitting up and looking at the youth.

"I am," answered our hero.

"Bless my soul! So you are!" cried Mr. Damon. "I was wondering who it could be. It's quite a coincidence. But I was in such a cloud of dust I couldn't make out who it was."

"You had your muffler open, and that made considerable dust," explained Tom.

"Was that it? Bless my existence! I thought something was wrong, but I couldn't tell what. I went over all the instructions in the book and those the agent told me, but I couldn't think of the right one. I tried all sorts of things to make less dust, but I couldn't. Then, bless my eyelashes, if the machine didn't stop just after I nearly ran into you. I tinkered over it for an hour or more before I could get it to going again. Then I ran into the tree. My doctor told me the machine would do my liver good, but, bless my happiness, I'd as soon be without a liver entirely as to do what I've done to-day. I am done with motor-cycling!"

A hopeful look came over Tom's face, but he said nothing, that is, not just then. In a little while Mr. Damon felt so much better that he said he would start for home.

"I'm afraid you'll have to leave your machine here," said Tom.

"You can send for it any time you want to," added Mr. Swift.

"Bless my hatband!" exclaimed Mr. Damon, who appeared to be very fond of blessing his vari-

ous organs and his articles of wearing apparel.
"Bless my hatband! I never want to see it again!
If you will be so kind as to keep it for me, I will
send a junk man after it. I will never spend anything on having it repaired. I am done with that
form of exercise—liver or no liver—doctor or no
doctor."

He appeared very determined. Tom quickly
made up his mind. Mr. Damon had gone to the
bathroom to get rid of some of the mud on his
hands and face.

"Father," said Tom earnestly, "may I buy that
machine of him?"

"What? Buy a broken motor-cycle?"

"I can easily fix it. It is a fine make, and in
good condition. I can repair it. I've wanted a
motor-cycle for some time, and here's a chance to
get a good one cheap."

"You don't need to do that," replied Mr. Swift.
"You have money enough to buy a new one if
you want it. I never knew you cared for them."

"I didn't, until lately. But I'd rather buy this
one and fix it up than get a new one. Besides, I
have an idea for a new kind of transmission, and
perhaps I can work it out on this machine."

"Oh, well, if you want it for experimental pur-
poses, I suppose it will be as good as any. Go

ahead, get it if you wish, but don't give too much for it."

"I'll not. I fancy I can get it cheap."

Mr. Damon returned to the living-room, where he had first been carried.

"I cannot thank you enough for what you have done for me," he said. "I might have lain there for hours. Bless my very existence! I have had a very narrow escape. Hereafter when I see anyone on a motor-cycle I shall turn my head away. The memory will be too painful," and he touched the plaster that covered a cut on his head.

"Mr. Damon," said Tom quickly, "will you sell me that motor-cycle?"

"Bless my finger rings! Sell you that mass of junk?"

"It isn't all junk," went on the young inventor. "I can easily fix it; though, of course," he added prudently, "it will cost something. How much would you want for it?"

"Well," replied Mr. Damon, "I paid two hundred and fifty dollars last week. I have ridden a hundred miles on it. That is at the rate of two dollars and a half a mile—pretty expensive riding. But if you are in earnest I will let you have the machine for fifty dollars, and then I fear that I will be taking advantage of you."

"I'll give you fifty dollars," said Tom quickly, and Mr. Damon exclaimed:

"Bless my liver—that is, if I have one. Do you mean it?"

Tom nodded. I'll fetch you the money right away," he said, starting for his room. He got the cash from a small safe he had arranged, which was fitted up with an ingenious burglar alarm, and was on his way downstairs when he heard his father call out:

"Here! What do you want? Go away from that shop! No one is allowed there!" and looking from an upper window, Tom saw his father running toward a stranger, who was just stepping inside the shop where Mr. Swift was constructing his turbine motor. Tom started as he saw that the stranger was the same black-mustached man whom he had noticed in the post-office, and, later, in the restaurant at Mansburg.

CHAPTER V

MR. SWIFT IS ALARMED

STUFFING the money which he intended to give to Mr. Damon in his pocket, Tom ran downstairs. As he passed through the living-room, intending to see what the disturbance was about, and, if necessary, aid his father, the owner of the broken motor-cycle exclaimed:

"What's the matter? What has happened? Bless my coat-tails, but is anything wrong?"

"I don't know," answered Tom. "There is a stranger about the shop, and my father never allows that. I'll be back in a minute."

"Take your time," advised the somewhat eccentric Mr. Damon. "I find my legs are a bit weaker than I suspected, and I will be glad to rest a while longer. Bless my shoelaces, but don't hurry!"

Tom went into the rear yard, where the shops, in a small cluster of buildings, were located. He saw his father confronting the man with the black mustache, and Mr. Swift was saying:

"What do you want? I allow no people to come in here unless I or my son invites them. Did you wish to see me?"

"Are you Mr. Barton Swift?" asked the man.

"Yes, that is my name."

"The inventor of the Swift safety lamp, and the turbine motor?"

At the mention of the motor Mr. Swift started.

"I am the inventor of the safety lamp you mention," he said stiffly, "but I must decline to talk about the motor. May I ask where you obtained your information concerning it?"

"Why, I am not at liberty to tell," went on the man. "I called to see if we could negotiate with you for the sale of it. Parties whom I represent——"

At that moment Tom plucked his father by the sleeve.

"Dad," whispered the youth, "I saw him in Mansburg. I think he is one of several who have been inquiring in Mr. Merton's shop about you and your patents. I wouldn't have anything to do with him until I found out more about him."

"Is that so?" asked Mr. Swift quickly. Then, turning to the stranger, he said: "My son tells me——"

But Mr. Swift got no further, for at that moment the stranger caught sight of Tom, whom he had not noticed before.

"Ha!" exclaimed the man. "I have forgotten something—an important engagement—will be back directly—will see you again, Mr. Swift— excuse the trouble I have put you to—I am in a great hurry," and before father or son could stop him, had they any desire to, the man turned and walked quickly from the yard.

Mr. Swift stood staring at him, and so did Tom. Then the inventor asked:

"Do you know that man? What about him, Tom? Why did he leave so hurriedly?"

"I don't know his name," replied Tom, "but I am suspicious regarding him, and I think he left because he suddenly recognized me." Thereupon he told his father of seeing the man in the post-office, and hearing the talk of the same individual and two companions in the restaurant.

"And so you think they are up to some mischief, Tom?" asked the parent when the son had finished.

"Well, I wouldn't go quite as far as that, but I think they are interested in your patents, and you ought to know whether you want them to be, or not."

"I most certainly do not—especially in the turbine motor. That is my latest invention, and, I think, will prove very valuable. But, though I have not mentioned it before, I expect to have trouble with it. Soon after I perfected it, with the exception of some minor details, I received word from a syndicate of rich men that I was infringing on a motor, the patent of which they controlled.

"This surprised me for two reasons. One was because I did not know that any one knew I had invented the motor. I had kept the matter secret, and I am at a loss to know how it leaked out. To prevent any further information concerning my plans becoming public, I sent you to Mansburg to-day. But it seems that the precaution was of little avail. Another matter of surprise was the information that I was infringing on the patent of some one else. I had a very careful examination made, and I found that the syndicate of rich men was wrong. I was not infringing. In fact, though the motor they have is somewhat like mine, there is one big difference—theirs does not work, while mine does. Their patents are worthless."

"Then what do you think is their object?"

"I think they want to get control of my invention of the turbine motor, Tom. That is what has been worrying me lately. I know these men to be unscrupulous, and, with plenty of money, they may make trouble for me."

"But can't you fight them in the courts?"

"Yes, I could do that. It is not as if I was a poor man, but I do not like lawsuits. I want to live quietly and invent things. I dislike litigation. However, if they force it on me I will fight!" exclaimed Mr. Swift determinedly.

"Do you think this man was one of the crowd of financiers?" asked Tom.

"It would be hard to say. I did not like his actions, and the fact that he sneaked in here, as if he was trying to get possession of some of my models or plans, makes it suspicious."

"It certainly does," agreed Tom. "Now, if we only knew his name we could——"

He suddenly paused in his remark and sprang forward. He picked up an envelope that had dropped where the stranger had been standing.

"The man lost this from his pocket, dad," said Tom eagerly. "It's a telegram. Shall we look at it?"

"I think we will be justified in protecting ourselves. Is the envelope open?"

"Yes."

"Then read the telegram."

Tom drew out a folded yellow slip of paper. It was a short message. He read:

" 'Anson Morse, Mansburg. See Swift to-day. Make offer. If not accepted do the best you can. Spare no effort. Don't give plans away.' "

"Is that all?" asked Mr. Swift.

"All except the signature."

"Who is the telegram signed by?"

"By Smeak & Katch," answered Tom.

"Those rascally lawyers!" exclaimed his father. "I was beginning to suspect this. That is the firm which represents the syndicate of wealthy men who are trying to get my turbine motor patents away from me. Tom, we must be on our guard! They will wage a fierce fight against me, for they have sunk many thousands of dollars in a worthless machine, and are desperate."

"We'll fight 'em!" cried Tom. "You and I, dad! We'll show 'em that the firm of Swift & Son is swift by name and swift by nature!"

"Good!" exclaimed the inventor. "I'm glad you feel that way about it, Tom. But we are going to have no easy task. Those men are rich and unscrupulous. We shall have to be on guard constantly. Let me have that telegram. It may come in useful. Now I must send word to Reid & Crawford, my attorneys in Washington, to be on the lookout. Matters are coming to a curious pass."

As Mr. Swift and his son started for the house, they met Mr. Damon coming toward them.

"Bless my very existence!" cried the eccentric man. "I was beginning to fear something had happened to you. I am glad that you are all right. I heard voices, and I imagined——"

"It's all right," Mr. Swift reassured him. "There was a stranger about my shop, and I never allow that. Do you feel well enough to go? If not we shall be glad to have you remain with us. We have plenty of room."

"Oh, thank you very much, but I must be going. I feel much better. Bless my gaiters, but I never will trust myself in even an automobile again! I will renounce gasolene from now on."

"That reminds me," spoke Tom. "I have the money for the motor-cycle," and he drew out the bills. "You are sure you will not regret your bargain, Mr. Damon? The machine is new, and needs only slight repairs. Fifty dollars is——"

"Tut, tut, young man! I feel as if I was getting the best of you. Bless my handkerchief! I hope you have no bad luck with it."

"I'll try and be careful," promised Tom with a smile as he handed over the money. "I am going to gear it differently and put some improvements on it. Then I will use it instead of my bicycle."

"It would have to be very much improved before I trusted myself on it again," declared **Mr.** Damon. "Well, I appreciate what you have done for me, and if at any time I can reciprocate the favor, I will only be too glad to do so. Bless **my** soul, though, I hope I don't have to rescue you from trying to climb a tree," and with a laugh, which showed that he had fully recovered from his mishap, he shook hands with father and son and left.

"A very nice man, Tom," commented Mr. Swift. "Somewhat odd and out of the ordinary, but a very fine character, for all that."

"That's what I say," added the son. "Now, dad, you'll see me scooting around the country on a motor-cycle. I've always wanted one, and now I have a bargain."

"Do you think you can repair it?"

"Of course, dad. I've done more difficult things than that. I'm going to take it apart now, and see what it needs."

"Before you do that, Tom, I wish you would take a telegram to town for me. I must wire my lawyers at once."

"Dad looks worried," thought Tom as he wheeled the broken motor-cycle into a machine shop, where he did most of his work. "Well, I don't blame him. But we'll get the best of those scoundrels yet!"

CHAPTER VI

AN INTERVIEW IN THE DARK

WHILE Mr. Swift was writing the message he wished his son to take to the village, the young mechanic inspected the motor-cycle he had purchased. Tom found that a few repairs would suffice to put it in good shape, though an entire new front wheel would be needed. The motor had not been damaged, as he ascertained by a test. Tom rode into town on his bicycle, and as he hurried along he noticed in the west a bank of ugly-looking clouds that indicated a shower.

"I'm in for a wetting before I get back," he mused, and he increased his speed, reaching the telegraph office shortly before seven o'clock.

"Think this storm will hold off until I get home?" asked Tom.

"I'm afraid not," answered the agent. "You'd better get a hustle on."

Tom sprinted off. It was getting dark rapidly, and when he was about a mile from home he felt several warm drops on his face.

45

"Here it comes!" exclaimed the youth. "Now for a little more speed!"

Tom pressed harder on the pedals, too hard, in fact, for an instant later something snapped, and the next he knew he was flying over the handlebars of the bicycle. At the same time there was a metallic, clinking sound.

"Chain's busted!" exclaimed the lad as he picked himself up out of the dust. "Well, wouldn't that jar you!" and he walked back to where, in the dusk, he could dimly discern his wheel.

The chain had come off the two sprockets and was lying to one side. Tom picked it up and ascertained by close observation that the screw and nut holding the two joining links together was lost.

"Nice pickle!" he murmured. "How am I going to find it in all this dust and darkness?" he asked himself disgustedly. "I'll carry an extra screw next time. No, I won't, either. I'll ride my motor-cycle next time. Well, I may as well give a look around. I hate to walk, if I can fix it and ride."

Tom had not spent more than two minutes looking about the dusty road, with the aid of matches, for the screw, when the rain suddenly began falling in a hard shower.

"Guess there's no use lingering here any longer," he remarked. "I'll push the wheel and run for home."

He started down the road in the storm and darkness. The highway soon became a long puddle of mud, through which he splashed, finding it more and more difficult every minute to push the bicycle in the thick, sticky clay.

Above the roar of the wind and the swishing of the rain he heard another sound. It was a steady "puff-puff," and then the darkness was cut by a glare of light.

"An automobile," said Tom aloud. "Guess I'd better get out of the way."

He turned to one side, but the auto, instead of passing him when it got to the place where he was, made a sudden stop.

"Want a ride?" asked the chauffeur, peering out from the side curtains which somewhat protected him from the storm. Tom saw that the car was a large, touring one. "Can I give you a lift?" went on the driver.

"Well, I've got my bicycle with me," explained the young inventor. "My chain's broken, and I've got a mile to go."

"Jump up in back," invited the man. "Leave your wheel here; I guess it will be safe."

"Oh, I couldn't do that," said Tom. "I don't

mind walking. I'm wet through now, and I can't get much wetter. "I'm much obliged, though."

"Well, I'm sorry, but I can hardly take you and the bicycle, too," continued the chauffeur.

"Certainly not," added a voice from the tonneau of the car. "We can't have a muddy bicycle in here. Who is that person, Simpson?"

"It's a young man," answered the driver.

"Is he acquainted around here?" went on the voice from the rear of the car. "Ask him if he is acquainted around here, Simpson."

Tom was wondering where he had heard that voice before. He had a vague notion that it was familiar.

"Are you acquainted around here?" obediently asked the man at the wheel.

"I live here," replied Tom.

"Ask him if he knows any one named Swift?" continued the voice from the tonneau, and the driver started to repeat it.

"I heard him," interrupted Tom. "Yes, I know a Mr. Swift"; but Tom, with a sudden resolve, and one he could hardly explain, decided that, for the present, he would not betray his own identity.

"Ask him if Mr. Swift is an inventor." Once more the unseen person spoke in the voice Tom was trying vainly to recall.

"Yes, he is an inventor," was the youth's answer.

"Do you know much about him? What are his habits? Does he live near his workshops? Does he keep many servants? Does he——"

The unseen questioner suddenly parted the side curtains and peered out at Tom, who stood in the muddy road, close to the automobile. At that moment there came a bright flash of lightning, illuminating not only Tom's face, but that of his questioner as well. And at the sight Tom started, no less than did the man. For Tom had recognized him as one of the three mysterious persons in the restaurant, and as for the man, he had also recognized Tom.

"Ah—er—um—is—— Why, it's you, isn't it?" cried the questioner, and he thrust his head farther out from between the curtains. My, what a storm!" he exclaimed as the rain increased. "So you know Mr. Swift, eh? I saw you to-day in Mansburg, I think. I have a good memory for faces. Do you work for Mr. Swift? If you do I may be able to——"

"I'm Tom Swift, son of Mr. Barton Swift," said Tom as quietly as he could.

"Tom Swift! His son!" cried the man, and he seemed much agitated. "Why, I thought—that is, Morse said—— Simpson, hurry back to Mansburg!" and with that, taking no more notice of Tom, the man in the auto hastily drew the curtains together.

The chauffeur threw in the gears and swung the ponderous machine to one side. The road was wide, and he made the turn skilfully. A moment later the car was speeding back the way it had come, leaving Tom standing on the highway, alone in the mud and darkness, with the rain pouring down in torrents.

CHAPTER VII

OFF ON A SPIN

Tom's first impulse was to run after the automobile, the red tail-light of which glowed through the blackness like a ruby eye. Then he realized that it was going from him at such a swift pace that it would be impossible to get near it, even if his bicycle was in working order.

"But if I had my motor-cycle I'd catch up to them," he murmured. "As it is, I must hurry home and tell dad. This is another link in the queer chain that seems to be winding around us. I wonder who that man was, and what he wanted by asking so many personal questions about dad?"

Trundling his wheel before him, with the chain dangling from the handle-bar, Tom splashed on through the mud and rain. It was a lonesome, weary walk, tired as he was with the happenings of the day, and the young inventor breathed a sigh of thankfulness as the lights of his home shone out in the mist of the storm. As he tramped up the steps of the side porch, his wheel bumping along ahead of him, a door was thrown open.

"Why, it's Tom!" exclaimed Mrs. Baggert. "Whatever happened to you?" and she hurried forward with kindly solicitude, for the housekeeper was almost a second mother to the youth.

"Chain broke," answered the lad laconically. "Where's dad?"

"Out in the shop, working at his latest invention, I expect. But are you hurt?"

"Oh, no. I fell easily. The mud was like a feather-bed, you know, except that it isn't so good for the clothes," and the young inventor looked down at his splashed and bedraggled garments.

Mr. Swift was very much surprised when Tom told him of the happening on the road, and related the conversation and the subsequent alarm of the man on learning Tom's identity.

"Who do you suppose he could have been?" asked Tom, when he had finished.

"I am pretty certain he was one of that crowd of financiers of whom Anson Morse seems to be a representative," said Mr. Swift. "Are you sure the man was one of those you saw in the restaurant?"

"Positive. I had a good look at him both times. Do you think he imagined he could come here and get possession of some of your secrets?"

"I hardly know what to think, Tom. But we will take every precaution. We will set the burglar alarm wires, which I have neglected for some time, as I fancied everything would be secure here. Then I will take my plans and the model of the turbine motor into the house. I'll run no chances to-night."

Mr. Swift, who was adjusting some of the new bolts that Tom had brought home that day, began to gather up his tools and material.

"I'll help you, dad," said Tom, and he began connecting the burglar alarm wires, there being an elaborate system of them about the house, shops and grounds.

Neither Tom nor his father slept well that night. Several times one or the other of them arose, thinking they heard unusual noises, but it was only some disturbance caused by the storm, and morning arrived without anything unusual having taken place. The rain still continued, and Tom, looking from his window and seeing the downpour, remarked:

"I'm glad of it!"

"Why?" asked his father, who was in the next room.

"Because I'll have a good excuse for staying in and working on my motor-cycle."

"But you must do some studying," declared

Mr. Swift. "I will hear you in mathematics right after breakfast."

"All right, dad. I guess you'll find I have my lessons."

Tom had graduated with honors from a local academy, and when it came to a question of going further in his studies, he had elected to continue with his father for a tutor, instead of going to college. Mr. Swift was a very learned man, and this arrangement was satisfactory to him, as it allowed Tom more time at home, so he could aid his father on the inventive work and also plan things for himself. Tom showed a taste for mechanics, and his father wisely decided that such training as his son needed could be given at home to better advantage than in a school or college.

Lessons over, Tom hurried to his own particular shop, and began taking apart the damaged motor-cycle.

"First I'll straighten the handle-bars, and then I'll fix the motor and transmission," he decided. "The front wheel I can buy in town, as this one would hardly pay for repairing."

Tom was soon busy with wrenches, hammers, pliers and screw-driver. He was in his element, and was whistling over his task. The motor he found in good condition, but it was not such an easy task as he had hoped to change the transmission. He had finally to appeal to his father, in order to get the right proportion between the back and front gears, for the motor-cycle was operated by a sprocket chain, instead of a belt drive, as is the case with some.

Mr. Swift showed Tom how to figure out the number of teeth needed on each sprocket, in order to get an increase of speed, and as there was a sprocket wheel from a disused piece of machinery available, Tom took that. He soon had it in place, and then tried the motor. To his delight the number of revolutions of the rear wheel were increased about fifteen per cent.

"I guess I'll make some speed," he announced to his father.

"But it will take more gasolene to run the motor; don't forget that. You know the great principle of mechanics—that you can't get out of a machine any more than you put into it, nor quite as much, as a matter of fact, for considerable is lost through friction."

"Well, then, I'll enlarge the gasolene tank," declared Tom. "I want to go fast when I'm going."

He reassembled the machine, and after several hours of work had it in shape to run, except that a front wheel was lacking.

"I think I'll go to town and get one," he re-marked. "The rain isn't quite so hard now."

In spite of his father's mild objections Tom went, using his bicycle, the chain of which he had quickly repaired. He found just the front wheel needed, and that night his motor-cycle was ready to run. But it was too dark to try it then, espe-cially as he had no good lantern, the one on the cycle having been smashed, and his own bicycle light not being powerful enough. So he had to postpone his trial trip until the next day.

He was up early the following morning, and went out for a spin before breakfast. He came back, with flushed cheeks and bright eyes, just as Mr. Swift and Mrs. Baggert were sitting down to the table.

"To Reedville and back," announced Tom proudly.

"What, a round trip of thirty miles!" exclaimed Mr. Swift.

"That's what!" declared his son. "I went like a greased pig most of the way. I had to slow up going through Mansburg, but the rest of the time I let it out for all it was worth.

"You must be careful," cautioned his father. "You are not an expert yet."

"No, I realize that. Several times, when I wanted to slow up, I began to back-pedal, forgetting that I wasn't on my bicycle. Then I thought to shut off the power and put on the brake. But it's glorious fun. I'm going out again as soon as I have something to eat. That is, unless you want me to help you, dad."

"No, not this morning. Learn to ride the motor-cycle. It may come in handy."

Neither Tom nor his father realized what an important part the machine was soon to play in their lives.

Tom went out for another spin after breakfast, and in a different direction. He wanted to see what the machine would do on a hill, and there was a long, steep one about five miles from home. The roads were in fine shape after the rain, and he speeded up the incline at a rapid rate.

"It certainly does eat up the road," the lad murmured. "I have improved this machine considerably. Wish I could take out a patent on it."

Reaching the crest of the slope, he started down the incline. He turned off part of the power, and was gliding along joyously, when from a cross-road he suddenly saw turn into the main highway a mule, drawing a ramshackle wagon, loaded with fence posts. Beside the animal walked an old colored man.

"I hope he gets out of the way in time," thought Tom. "He's moving as slow as molasses, and

I'm going a bit faster than I like. Guess I'll shut off and put on the brakes."

The mule and wagon were now squarely across the road. Tom was coming nearer and nearer. He turned the handle-grip, controlling the supply of gasolene, and to his horror he found that it was stuck. He could not stop the motor-cycle!

"Look out! Look out!" cried Tom to the negro. "Get out of the way! I can't stop! Let me pass you!"

The darky looked up. He saw the approaching machine, and he seemed to lose possession of his senses.

"Whoa, Boomerang!" cried the negro. "Whoa! Suffin's gwine t' happen!"

"That's what!" muttered Tom desperately, as he saw that there was not room for him to pass without going into the ditch, a proceeding that would mean an upset. "Pull out of the way!" he yelled again.

But either the driver could not understand, or did not appreciate the necessity. The mule stopped and reared up. The colored man hurried to the head of the animal to quiet it.

"Whoa, Boomerang! Jest yo' stand still!" he said.

Tom, with a great effort, managed to twist the grip and finally shut off the gasolene. But it was too late. He struck the darky with the front wheel. Fortunately the youth had managed to somewhat reduce his speed by a quick application of the brake, or the result might have been serious. As it was, the colored man was gently lifted away from the mule's head and tossed into the long grass in the ditch. Tom, by a great effort, succeeded in maintaining his seat in the saddle, and then, bringing the machine to a stop, he leaped off and turned back.

The colored man was sitting up, looking dazed.

"Whoa, Boomerang!" he murmured. "Suffin's happened!"

But the mule, who had quieted down, only waggled his ears lazily, and Tom, ready to laugh, now that he saw he had not committed manslaughter, hurried to where the colored man was sitting.

CHAPTER VIII

SUSPICIOUS ACTIONS

"Are you hurt?" asked Tom as he leaned his motor-cycle against the fence and stood beside the negro.

"Hurt?" repeated the darky. "I'se killed, dat's what I is! I ain't got a whole bone in mah body! Good landy, but I suttinly am in a awful state! Would yo' mind tellin' me if dat ar' mule am still alive?"

"Of course he is," answered Tom. "He isn't hurt a bit. But why can't you turn around and look for yourself?"

"No, sah! No, indeedy, sah!" replied the colored man. "Yo' doan't catch dis yeah nigger lookin' around!"

"Why not?"

"Why not? 'Cause I'll tell yo' why not. I'm so stiff an' I'm so nearly broke t' pieces, dat if I turn mah head around it suah will twist offen mah body. No, sah! No, indeedy, sah, I ain't

60

gwine t' turn 'round. But am yo' suah dat mah mule Boomerang ain't hurted?"

"No, he's not hurt a bit, and I'm sure you are not. I didn't strike you hard, for I had almost stopped my machine. Try to get up. I'm positive you'll find yourself all right. I'm sorry it happened."

"Oh, dat's all right. Doan't mind me," went on the colored man. "It was mah fault fer gittin in de road. But dat mule Boomerang am suttinly de most outrageous quadraped dat ever circumlocuted."

"Why do you call him Boomerang?" asked Tom, wondering if the negro really was hurt.

"What fo' I call him Boomerang? Did yo' eber see dem Australian black mans what go around wid a circus t'row dem crooked sticks dey calls boomerangs?"

"Yes, I've seen them."

"Well, Boomerang, mah mule, am jest laik dat. He's crooked, t' begin wid, an' anudder t'ing, yo' can't never tell when yo' start him whar he's gwine t' land up. Dat's why I calls him Boomerang."

"I see. It's a very proper name. But why don't you try to get up?"

"Does yo' t'ink I can?"

"Sure. Try it. By the way, what's your name?"

"My name? Why I was christened Eradicate Andrew Jackson Abraham Lincoln Sampson, but folks most ginnerally calls me Eradicate Sampson, an' some doan't eben go to dat length. Dey jest calls me Rad, fo' short."

"Eradicate," mused Tom. "That's a queer name, too. Why were you called that?"

"Well, yo' see I eradicates de dirt. I'm a cleaner an' a whitewasher by profession, an' somebody gib me dat name. Dey said it were fitten an' proper, an' I kept it eber sence. Yais, sah, I'se Eradicate Sampson, at yo' service. Yo' ain't got *no* chicken coops yo' wants cleaned out, has yo'? Or any stables or fences t' whitewash? I guarantees satisfaction."

"Well, I might find some work for you to do," replied the young inventor, thinking this would be as good a means as any of placating the darky. "But come, now, try and see if you can't stand. I don't believe I broke any of your legs."

"I guess not. I feels better now. Where am *dat* work yo' was speakin' ob?" and Eradicate Sampson, now that there seemed to be a prospect of earning money, rose quickly and easily.

"Why, you're all right!" exclaimed Tom, glad

to find that the accident had had no serious consequences.

"Yais, sah, I guess I be. Whar did yo' say yo' had some whitewashin' t' do?"

"No place in particular, but there is always something that needs doing at our house. If you call I'll give you a job."

"Yais, sah, I'll be sure to call," and Eradicate walked back to where Boomerang was patiently waiting.

Tom told the colored man how to find the Swift home, and was debating with himself whether he ought not to offer Eradicate some money as compensation for knocking him into the air, when he noticed that the negro was tying one wheel of his wagon fast to the body of the vehicle with a rope.

"What are you doing that for?" asked Tom.

"Got to, t' git downhill wid dis load ob fence posts," was the answer. "Ef I didn't it would be right on to de heels ob Boomerang, an' whenever he feels anyt'ing on his heels he does act wuss dan a circus mule."

"But why don't you use your brake? I see you have one on the wagon. Use the brake to hold back going downhill."

" 'Scuse me, Mistah Swift, 'scuse me!" exclaimed Eradicate quickly. "But yo' doan't know

dat brake. It's wuss dan none at all. It doan't
work, fer a fact. No, indeedy, sah. I'se got to
rope de wheel."

Tom was interested at once. He made an examination of the brake, and soon saw why it
would not hold the wheels. The foot lever was
not properly connected with the brake bar. It
was a simple matter to adjust it by changing a
single bolt, and this Tom did with tools he took
from the bag on his motor-cycle. The colored
man looked on in open-mouthed amazement, and
even Boomerang peered lazily around, as if taking
an interest in the proceedings.

"There," said Tom at length, as he tightened
the nut. "That brake will work now, and hold
the wagon on any hill. You won't need to rope
the wheel. You didn't have the right leverage
on it."

" 'Scuse me, Mistah Swift, but what's dat yo'
said?" and Eradicate leaned forward to listen
deferentially.

"I said you didn't have the right leverage."

"No, sah, Mistah Swift, 'scuse me, but yo' made
a slight mistake. I ain't never had no liverage
on dis yeah wagon. It ain't dat kind ob a wagon.
I onct drove a livery rig, but dat were some years
ago. I ain't worked fo' de livery stable in some
time now. Dat's why I know dere ain't no livery

on dis wagon. Yo'll 'scuse me, but yo' am slightly mistaken."

"All right," rejoined Tom with a laugh, not thinking it worth while to explain what he meant by the lever force of the brake rod. "Let it go at that. Livery or no livery, your brake will work now. I guess you're all right. Now don't forget to come around and do some whitewashing," and seeing that the colored man was able to mount to the seat and start off Boomerang, who seemed to have deep-rooted objections about moving, Tom wheeled his motor-cycle back to the road.

Eradicate Sampson drove his wagon a short distance and then suddenly applied the brake. It stopped short, and the mule looked around as if surprised.

"It suah do work, Mistah Swift!" called the darky to Tom, who was waiting the result of his little repair job. "It suah do work!"

"I'm glad of it."

"Mah golly! But yo' am suttinly a conjureman when it comes t' fixin' wagons! Did yo' eber work fer a blacksmith?"

"No, not exactly. Well, good-by, Eradicate. I'll look for you some day next week."

With that Tom leaped on his machine and speeded off ahead of the colored man and his rig.

As he passed the load of fence posts the youth heard Eradicate remark in awestricken tones:

"Mah golly! He suttinly go laik de wind! An' t' t'ink dat I were hit by dat monstrousness machine, an' not hurted! Mah golly! T'ings am suttinly happenin'! G'lang, Boomerang!"

"This machine has more possibilities in it than I suspected," mused Tom. "But one thing I've got to change, and that is the gasolene and spark controls. I don't like them the way they are. I want a better leverage, just as Eradicate needed on his wagon. I'll fix them, too, when I get home."

He rode for several hours, until he thought it was about dinner time, and then, heading the machine toward home, he put on all the speed possible, soon arriving where his father was at work in the shop.

"Well, how goes it?" asked Mr. Swift with a smile as he looked at the flushed face of his son.

"Fine, dad! I scooted along in great shape. Had an adventure, too."

"You didn't meet any more of those men, did you? The men who are trying to get my invention?" asked Mr. Swift apprehensively.

"No, indeed, dad. I simply had a little run-in with a chap named Eradicate Andrew Jackson Abraham Lincoln Sampson, otherwise known as

Rad Sampson, and I engaged him to do some whitewashing for us. We do need some whitewashing done, don't we, dad?"

"What's that?" asked Mr. Swift, thinking his son was joking.

Then Tom told of the happening.

"Yes, I think I can find some work for Eradicate to do," went on Mr. Swift. "There is some dirt in the boiler shop that needs eradicating, and I think he can do it. But dinner has been waiting some time. We'll go in now, or Mrs. Baggert will be out after us."

Father and son were soon at the table, and Tom was explaining what he meant to do to improve his motor-cycle. His father offered some suggestions regarding the placing of the gasolene lever.

"I'd put it here," he said, and with his pencil he began to draw a diagram on the white tablecloth.

"Oh, my goodness me, Mr. Swift!" exclaimed Mrs. Baggert. "Whatever are you doing?" and she sprang up in some alarm.

"What's the matter? Did I upset my tea?" asked the inventor innocently.

"No; but you are soiling a clean tablecloth. Pencil-marks are so hard to get out. Take a piece of paper, please."

"Oh, is that all?" rejoined Mr. Swift with a smile. "Well, Tom, here is the way I would do that," and substituting the back of an envelope for the tablecloth, he continued the drawing.

Tom was looking over his father's shoulder interestedly, when Mrs. Baggert, who was taking off some of the dinner dishes, suddenly asked:

"Are you expecting a visitor, Mr. Swift?"

"A visitor? No. Why?" asked the inventor quickly.

"Because I just saw a man going in the machine shop," went on the housekeeper.

"A man! In the machine shop!" exclaimed Tom, rising from his chair. Mr. Swift also got up, and the two hurried from the house. As they reached the yard they saw a man emerging from the building where Mr. Swift was constructing his turbine motor. The man had his back turned toward them and seemed to be sneaking around, as though desirous of escaping observation.

"What do you want?" called Mr. Swift.

The man turned quickly. At the sight of Mr. Swift and Tom he made a jump to one side and got behind a big packing-box.

"That's queer," spoke Tom. "I wonder what he wants?"

"I'll soon see," rejoined Mr. Swift, and he started on a run toward where the man was hiding. Tom followed his father, and as the two inventors reached the box the man sprang from behind it and down the yard to a lane that passed in back of the Swift house. As he ran he was seen to stuff some papers in his pocket.

"My plans! He's stolen some of my plans!" cried Mr. Swift. "Catch him, Tom!"

Tom ran after the stranger, whose curious actions had roused their suspicions, while Mr. Swift entered the motor shop to ascertain whether anything had been stolen.

CHAPTER IX

A FRUITLESS PURSUIT

Down through the yard Tom speeded, in and out among the buildings, looking on every side for a sight of the bold stranger. No one was to be seen.

"He can't be very far ahead." thought Tom. "I ought to catch him before he gets to the woods. If he reaches there he has a good chance of getting away."

There was a little patch of trees just back of the inventor's house, not much of a woods, perhaps, but that is what they were called.

"I wonder if he was some ordinary tramp, looking for what he could steal, or if he was one of the gang after dad's invention?" thought Tom as he sprinted ahead.

By this time the youth was clear of the group of buildings and in sight of a tall, board fence, which surrounded the Swift estate on three sides. Here and there, along the barrier, were piled old packing-cases, so that it would be easy for a fugitive to leap upon one of them and so get over the fence. Tom thought of this possibility in a moment.

"I guess he got over ahead of me," the lad exclaimed, and he peered sharply about. "I'll catch him on the other side!"

At that instant Tom tripped over a plank and went down full length, making quite a racket. When he picked himself up he was surprised to see the man he was after dart from inside a big box and start for the fence, near a point where there were some packing-cases piled up, making a good approach to the barrier. The fugitive had been hiding, waiting for a chance to escape, and Tom's fall had alarmed him.

"Here! Hold on there! Come back!" cried the youth as he recovered his wind and leaped forward.

But the man did not stay. With a bound he was up on the pile of boxes, and the next moment he was poised on top of the fence. Before leaping down on the other side, a jump at which even a practiced athlete might well hesitate, the fleeing stranger paused and looked back. Tom gazed at him and recognized the man in an instant. He was the third of the mysterious trio whom the lad had seen in the Mansburg restaurant.

"Wait a minute! What do you want sneaking around here?" shouted Tom as he ran forward. The man returned no answer, and an instant later disappeared from view on the other side of the fence.

"He jumped down!" thought Tom. "A big leap, too. Well, I've got to follow. This is a queer proceeding. First one, then the second, and now the third of those men seem determined to get something here. I wonder if this one succeeded? I'll soon find out."

The lad was up on the pile of packing-cases and over the fence in almost record time. He caught a glimpse of the fugitive running toward the woods. Then the boy leaped down, jarring himself considerably, and took after the man.

But though Tom was a good runner he was handicapped by the fact that the man had a start of him, and also by the fact that the stranger had had a chance to rest while hiding for the second time in the big box, while Tom had kept on running. So it is no great cause for wonder that Mr. Swift's son found himself being distanced.

Once, twice he called on the fleeing one to halt, but the man paid no attention, and did not even turn around. Then the youth wisely concluded to save his wind for running. He did his best, but was chagrined to see the man reach the woods ahead of him.

"I've lost him now," thought Tom. "Well, there's no help for it."

Still he did not give up, but kept on through the patch of trees. On the farther side was Lake Carlopa, a broad and long sheet of water.

"If he doesn't know the lake's there," thought our hero, "he may keep straight on. The water will be sure to stop him, and I can catch him. But what will I do with him after I get him? That's another question. I guess I've got a right to demand to know what he was doing around our place, though."

But Tom need not have worried on this score. He could hear the fugitive ahead of him, and marked his progress by the crackling of the underbrush.

"I'm almost up to him," exulted the young inventor. Then, at the same moment, he caught sight of the man running, and a glimpse of the sparkling water of Lake Carlopa. "I've got him! I've got him!" Tom almost cried aloud in his excitement. "Unless he takes to the water and swims for it, I've got him!"

But Tom did not reckon on a very simple matter, and that was the possibility of the man having a boat at hand. For this is just what hap-

pened. Reaching the lake shore the fugitive with
a final spurt managed to put considerable distance
between himself and Tom. Drawn up on the
beach was a little motor-boat. In this, after he
had pushed it from shore, the stranger leaped.
It was the work of but a second to set the engine
in motion, and as Tom reached the edge of the
woods and started across the narrow strip of sand
and gravel that was between the water and the
trees, he saw the man steering his craft toward
the middle of the lake.

"Well—I'll—be—jiggered!" exclaimed the
youth. "Who would have thought he'd have a
motor-boat waiting for him? He planned this
well."

There was nothing to do but turn back. Tom
had a small rowboat and a sailing skiff on the
lake, but his boathouse was some distance away,
and even if he could get one of his craft out, the
motor-boat would soon distance it.

"He's gone!" thought the searcher regretfully.

The man in the motor-boat did not look back.
He sat in the bow, steering the little craft right
across the broadest part of Lake Carlopa.

"I wonder where he came from, and where he's
going?" mused Tom. "That's a boat I never saw
on this lake before. It must be a new one. Well,
there's no help for it, I've got to go back and tell

dad I couldn't catch him." And with a last look
at the fugitive, who, with his boat, was becoming
smaller and smaller every minute, Tom turned
and retraced his steps.

CHAPTER X

OFF TO ALBANY

"Did you catch him, Tom?" asked Mr. Swift eagerly when his son returned, but the inventor needed but a glance at the lad's despondent face to have his question answered without words. "Never mind," he added, "there's not much harm done, fortunately."

"Did he get anything? Any of your plans or models, dad?"

"No; not as far as I can discover. My papers in the shop were not disturbed, but it looked as if the turbine model had been moved. The only thing missing seems to be a sheet of unimportant calculations. Luckily I had my most valuable drawings in the safe in the house."

"Yet that man seemed to be putting papers in his pocket, dad. Maybe he made copies of some of your drawings."

"That's possible, Tom, and I admit it worries me. I can't imagine who that man is, unless——"

"Why, he's one of the three men I saw in

Mansburg in the restaurant," said Tom eagerly.
"Two of them tried to get information here, and
now the third one comes. He got away in a
motor-boat," and Tom told how the fugitive escaped.

Mr. Swift looked worried. It was not the first
time attempts had been made to steal his inventions, but on this occasion a desperate and well-
organized plan appeared to be on foot.

"What do you think they are up to, dad?"
asked Tom.

"I think they are trying to get hold of my turbine motor, Tom. You know I told you that
the financiers were disappointed in the turbine
motor they bought of another inventor. It does
not work. To get back the money they spent in
building an expensive plant they must have a
motor that is successful. Hence their efforts to
get control of mine. I don't know whether I told
you or not, but some time ago I refused a very
good offer for certain rights in my invention. I
knew it was worth more. The offer came through
Smeak & Katch, the lawyers, and when I refused
it they seemed much disappointed. I think now
that this same firm, and the financiers who have
employed them, are trying by all the means in
their power to get possession of my ideas, if not
the invention and model itself."

"What can you do, dad?"

"Well, I must think. I certainly must take some means to protect myself. I have had trouble before, but never any like this. I did not think those men would be so unscrupulous."

"Do you know their names?"

"No, only from that telegram we found; the one which the first stranger dropped. One of them must be Anson Morse. Who the others are I don't know. But now I must make some plans to foil these sharpers. I may have to call on you for help, Tom."

"And I'll be ready any time you call on me, dad," responded Tom, drawing himself up. "Can I do anything for you right away?"

"No; I must think out a plan."

"Then I am going to change my motor-cycle a bit. I'll put some more improvements on it."

"And I will write some letters to my lawyers in Washington and ask their advice."

It took Tom the remainder of that day, and part of the next, to arrange the gasolene and spark control of his machine to his satisfaction. He had to make two small levers and some connecting rods. This he did in his own particular machine shop, which was fitted up with a lathe and other apparatus. The lathe was run by power coming from a small engine, which was operated

by an engineer, an elderly man to whom Mr. Swift
had given employment for many years. He was
Garret Jackson, and he kept so close to his engine
and boiler-room that he was seldom seen outside
of it except when the day's work was done.

One afternoon, a few days after the unsuccessful chase after the fugitive had taken place, Tom
went out for a spin on his motor-cycle. He found
that the machine worked much better, and was
easier to control. He rode about fifteen miles
away from home, and then returned. As he entered the yard he saw, standing on the drive, a
ramshackle old wagon, drawn by a big mule,
which seemed, at the time Tom observed him, to
be asleep.

"I'll wager that's Boomerang," said Tom aloud,
and the mule opened its eyes, wiggled its ears and
started forward.

"Whoa dar, Boomerang!" exclaimed a voice,
and Eradicate Sampson hurried around the corner
of the house. "Dat's jest laik yo'," went on the
colored man. "Movin' when yo' ain't wanted to."
Then, as he caught sight of Tom, he exclaimed.
"Why, if it ain't young Mistah Swift! Good
landy! But dat livery brake yo' done fixed on mah
wagon suttinly am fine. Ah kin go down de steep-
est hill widout ropin' de wheel."

"Glad of it," replied Tom. "Did you come to do some work?"

"Yais, sah, I done did. I found I had some time t' spah, an' thinks I dere might be some whitewashin' I could do. Yo' see, I lib only 'bout two mile from heah."

"Well, I guess you can do a few jobs," said Tom. "Wait here."

He hunted up his father, and obtained permission to set Eradicate at work cleaning out a chicken house and whitewashing it. The darky was soon at work. A little later Tom passing saw him putting the whitewash on thick. Eradicate stopped at the sight of Tom, and made some curious motions.

"What's the matter, Rad?" asked the young inventor.

"Why, de whitewash done persist in runnin' down de bresh handle an' inter mah sleeve. I'm soakin' wet from it now, an' I has t' stop ebery onct in a while 'case mah sleeve gits full."

Tom saw what the trouble was. The white fluid did run down the long brush handle in a small rivulet. Tom had once seen a little rubber device on a window-cleaning brush that worked well, and he decided to try it for Eradicate.

"Wait a minute," Tom advised. "I think I can stop that for you."

The colored man was very willing to take a
rest, but it did not last long, for Tom was soon
back at the chicken coop. He had a small rubber
disk, with a hole in the center, the size of the
brush handle. Slipping the disk over the wood,
he pushed it about half way along, and then, hand-
ing the brush back to the negro, told him to try
it that way.

"Did yo' done put a charm on mah bresh?"
asked Eradicate somewhat doubtfully.

"Yes, a sort of hoodoo charm. Try it now."

The darky dipped his brush in the pail of whitewash, and then began to spread the disinfectant
on the sides of the coop near the top. The surplus
fluid started to run down the handle, but, meeting
the piece of rubber, came no farther, and dripped
off on the ground. It did not run down the sleeve
of Eradicate.

"Well, I 'clar t' goodness! Dat suttinly am a
mighty fine charm!" cried the colored man. "Yo'
suah am a pert gen'men, all right. Now I kin
work widout stoppin' t' empty mah sleeve ob
lime juice ebery minute. I'se suttinly obliged t'
yo'."

"You're welcome, I'm sure," replied Tom. "I
think some day I'll invent a machine for whitewashing, and then——"

"Doan't do dat! Doan't do dat!" begged

Eradicate earnestly. "Dis, an' makin' dirt disappear, am de only perfessions I got. Doan't go 'ventin' no machine, Mistah Swift."

"All right. I'll wait until you get rich."

"Ha, ha! Den yo' gwine t' wait a pow'ful long time," chuckled Eradicate as he went on with his whitewashing.

Tom went into the house. He found his father busy with some papers at his desk.

"Ah, it's you, is it, Tom?" asked the inventor, looking up. "I was just wishing you would come in."

"What for, dad?"

"Well, I have quite an important mission for you. I want you to go on a journey."

"A journey? Where?"

"To Albany. You see, I've been thinking over matters, and I have been in correspondence with my lawyers in regard to my turbine motor. I must take measures to protect myself. You know I have not yet taken out a complete patent on the machine. I have not done so because I did not want to put my model on exhibition in Washington. I was afraid some of those unscrupulous men would take advantage of me. Another point was that I had not perfected a certain device that goes on the motor. That objection is now removed, and I am ready to send my model to Washington, and take out the complete patent."

"But I thought you said you wanted me to go to Albany."

"So I do. I will explain. I have just had a letter from Reid & Crawford, my Washington attorneys. Mr. Crawford, the junior member of the firm, will be in Albany this week on some law business. He agrees to receive my model and some papers there, and take them back to Washington with him. In this way they will be well protected. You see, I have to be on my guard, and if I send the model to Albany, instead of the national capital, I may throw the plotters off the track, for I feel that they are watching every move I make. As soon as you or I should start for Washington they would be on our trail. But you can go to Albany unsuspected. Mr. Crawford will wait for you there. I want you to start day after to-morrow."

"All right, dad. I can start now, if you say, so."

"No, there is no special need for haste. I have some matters to arrange. You might go to the station and inquire about trains to the State capital."

"Am I going by train?"

"Certainly. How else could you go?"

There was a look of excitement in Tom's eyes. He had a sudden idea.

"Dad," he exclaimed, "why couldn't I go on my motor-cycle?"

"Your motor-cycle?"

"Yes. I could easily make the trip on it in one day. The roads are good, and I would enjoy it. I can carry the model back of me on the saddle. It is not very large."

"Well," said Mr. Swift slowly, for the idea was a new one to him, "I suppose that part would be all right. But you have not had much experience riding a motor-cycle. Besides, you don't know the roads."

"I can inquire. Will you let me go, dad?"

Mr. Swift appeared to hesitate.

"It will be fine!" went on Tom. "I would enjoy the trip, and there's another thing. If we want to keep this matter secret the best plan would be to let me go on my machine. If those men are on the watch, they will not think that I have the model. They will think I'm just going for a pleasure jaunt."

"There's something in that," admitted Mr. Swift, and Tom, seeing that his father was favorably inclined, renewed his arguments, until the inventor finally agreed.

"It will be a great trip!" exclaimed Tom. "I'll

go all over my machine now, to see that it's in good shape. You get your papers and model ready, dad, and I'll take them to Albany for you. The motor-cycle will come in handy."

But had Tom only known the dangers ahead of him, and the r·sks he was to run, he would not have whistled so light heartedly as he went over every nut and bolt on his machine.

Two days later, the valuable model, having been made into a convenient package, and wrapped in water-proof paper, was fastened back of the saddle on the motor-cycle. Tom carefully pinned in an inside pocket the papers which were to be handed to Mr. Crawford. He was to meet the lawyer at a hotel in Albany.

"Now take care of yourself, Tom," cautioned his father as he bade him good-by. "Don't try to make speed, as there is no special rush. And, above all, don't lose anything."

"I'll not, dad," and with a wave of his hand to Mr. Swift and the housekeeper, who stood in the door to see him off, Tom jumped into the saddle, started the machine, and then, after sufficient momentum had been attained, he turned on the gasolene and set the spark lever. With rattles and bangs, which were quickly subdued by the muffler, the machine gathered speed. Tom was off for Albany.

CHAPTER XI

A VINDICTIVE TRAMP

THOUGH Tom's father had told him there wa̸,
no necessity for any great speed, the young inventor could not resist the opportunity for pushing his machine to the limit. The road was a
level one and in good condition, so the motor-
cycle fairly flew along. The day was pleasant, a
warm sun shining overhead, and it was evident
that early summer was crowding spring rather
closely.

"This is glorious!" exclaimed Tom aloud as
he spun along. "I'm glad I persuaded dad to
let me take this trip. It was a great idea. Wish
Ned Newton was along, though. He'd be company for me, but, as Ned would say, there are
two good reasons why he can't come. One is
he has to work in the bank, and the other is that
he has no motor-cycle."

Tom swept past house after house along the
road, heading in the opposite direction from that

in which lay the town of Shopton and the city of Mansburg. For several miles Tom's route would lie through a country district. The first large town he would reach would be Centreford. He planned to get lunch there, and he had brought a few sandwiches with him to eat along the road in case he became hungry before he reached the place.

"I hope the package containing the model doesn't jar off," mused the lad as he reached behind to make sure that the precious bundle was safe. "Dad would be in a bad way if that should disappear. And the papers, too." He put his hand to his inner pocket to feel that they were secure. Coming to a little down-grade, Tom shut off some of the power, the new levers he had arranged to control the gasolene and spark working well.

"I think I'll take the old wood road and pass through Pompville," Tom decided, after covering another mile or two. He was approaching a division in the highway. "It's a bit sandy," he went on, "and the going will be heavy, but it will be a good chance to test my machine. Besides, I'll save five miles, and, while I don't have to hurry, I may need time on the other end. I'd rather arrive in Albany a little before dusk than after dark. I can deliver the model and papers and have a good night's sleep before starting back. So the old wood road it will be."

The wood road, as Tom called it, was a seldom used highway, which, originally, was laid out for just what the name indicated, to bring wood from the forest. With the disappearance of most of the trees the road became more used for ordinary traffic between the towns of Pompville and Edgefield. But when the State built a new highway connecting these two places the old road fell into disuse, though it was several miles shorter than the new turnpike.

He turned from the main thoroughfare, and was soon spinning along the sandy stretch, which was shaded with trees that in some places met overhead, forming a leafy arch. It was cool and pleasant, and Tom liked it.

"It isn't as bad as I thought," he remarked. "The sand is pretty thick, but this machine of mine appears to be able to crawl through it."

Indeed, the motor-cycle was doing remarkably well, but Tom found that he had to turn on full power, for the big rubber wheels went deep into the soft soil. Along Tom rode, picking out the firmest places in the road. He was so intent on this that he did not pay much attention to what was immediately ahead of him, knowing that he was not very likely to meet other vehicles or pedestrians. He was considerably startled therefore when, as he went around a turn in the highway where the bushes grew thick, right down to the edge of the road, to see a figure emerge from the underbrush and start across the path. So quickly did the man appear that Tom was almost upon him in an instant, and even though the young inventor shut off the power and applied the brake, the front wheel hit the man and knocked him down.

"What's the matter with you? What are you trying to do—kill me? Why don't you ring a bell or blow a horn when you're coming?" The man had sprung up from the soft sand where the wheel from the motor-cycle had sent him and faced Tom angrily. Then the rider, who had quickly dismounted, saw that his victim was a ragged tramp.

"I'm sorry," began Tom. "You came out of the bushes so quickly that I didn't have a chance to warn you. Did I hurt you much?"

"Well, youse might have. 'Tain't your fault dat youse didn't," and the tramp began to brush the dirt from his ragged coat. Tom was instantly struck by a curious fact. The tramp in his second remarks used language more in keeping with his character, whereas, in his first surprise and anger, he had talked much as any other person would. "Youse fellers ain't got no right t' ride dem machines like lightnin' along de roads," the ragged chap went on, and he still clung to the use of words and expressions current among his fraternity. Tom wondered at it, and then, ascribing the use of the better language to the fright caused by being hit by the machine, the lad thought no more about it at the time. There was occasion, however, when he attached more meaning to it.

"I'm very sorry," went on Tom. "I'm sure I didn't mean to. You see, I was going quite slowly, and——"

"You call dat slow, when youse hit me an' knocked me down?" demanded the tramp. "I'd oughter have youse arrested, dat's what, an' I would if dere was a cop handy."

"I wasn't going at all fast," said Tom, a little nettled that his conciliatory words should be so rudely received. "If I had been going full speed I'd have knocked you fifty feet."

"It's a good thing. Cracky, den I'm glad dat youse wasn't goin' like dat," and the tramp seemed somewhat confused. This time Tom looked at him more closely, for the change in his language had been very plain. The fellow seemed uneasy, and turned his face away. As he did so Tom caught a glimpse of what he was sure was a false beard. It was altogether too well-kept a beard to be a natural one for such a dirty tramp as this one appeared to be.

"That fellow's disguised!" Tom thought. "He's playing a part. I wonder if I'd better take chances and spring it on him that I'm on to his game?"

Then the ragged man spoke again:

"I s'pose it was part my fault, cully. I didn't know dat any guy was comin' along on one of dem buzz-machines, or I'd been more careful. I don't s'pose youse meant to upset me?" and he looked at Tom more boldly. This time his words seemed so natural, and his beard, now that Tom took a second look at it, so much a part of himself, that the young inventor wondered if he could have been mistaken in his first surmise.

"Perhaps he was once a gentleman, and has turned tramp because of hard luck," thought Tom. "That would account for him using good language at times. Guess I'd better keep still." Then to the tramp he said: "I'm sure I didn't mean to hit you. I admit I wasn't looking where I was going, but I never expected to meet any one on this road. I certainly didn't expect to see a——"

He paused in some confusion. He was about to use the term "tramp," and he hesitated, not knowing how it would be received by his victim.

"Oh, dat's all right, cully. Call me a tramp— I know dat's what youse was goin' t' say. I'm used t' it. I've been a hobo so many years now dat I don't mind. De time was when I was a decent chap, though. But I'm a tramp now. Say, youse couldn't lend me a quarter, could youse?"

He approached closer to Tom, and looked quickly up and down the road. The highway was deserted, nor was there any likelihood that any one would come along. Tom was somewhat apprehensive, for the tramp was a burly specimen. The young inventor, however, was not so much alarmed at the prospect of a personal encounter, as that he feared he might be robbed, not only of his money, but the valuable papers and model he carried. Even if the tramp was content with taking his money, it would mean that Tom would have to go back home for more, and so postpone his trip.

So it was with no little alarm that he watched the ragged man coming nearer to him. Then a bright idea came into Tom's head. He quickly shifted his position so that he brought the heavy motor-cycle between the man and himself. He resolved, if the tramp showed a disposition to attack him, to push the machine over on him, and this would give Tom a chance to attack the thief to better advantage. However, the "hobo" showed no evidence of wanting to resort to highwayman methods. He paused a short distance from the machine, and said admiringly:

"Dat's a pretty shebang youse has."

"Yes, it's very fair," admitted Tom, who was not yet breathing easily.

"Kin youse go far on it?"

"Two hundred miles a day, easily."

"Fer cats' sake! An' I can't make dat ridin' on de blind baggage; but dat's 'cause I gits put off so much. But say, is youse goin' to let me have dat quarter? I need it, honest I do. I ain't had nuttin' t' eat in two days."

The man's tone was whining. Surely he seemed like a genuine tramp, and Tom felt a little sorry for him. Besides, he felt that he owed him something for the unceremonious manner in which he had knocked the fellow down. Tom reached his hand in his pocket for some change, taking care to keep the machine between himself and the tramp.

"Are youse goin' far on dat rig-a-ma-jig?" went on the man as he looked carefully over the motor-cycle.

"To Albany," answered Tom, and the moment the words were out of his mouth he wished he could recall them. All his suspicions regarding the tramp came back to him. But the ragged chap appeared to attach no significance to them.

"Albany? Dat's in Jersey, ain't it?" he asked.

"No, it's in New York," replied Tom, and then, to change the subject, he pulled out a half-dollar and handed it to the man. As he did so Tom noticed that the tramp had tattooed on the little finger of his left hand a blue ring.

"Dat's de stuff! Youse is a reg'lar millionaire, youse is!" exclaimed the tramp, and his manner seemed in earnest. "I'll remember youse, I will. What's your name, anyhow, cully?"

"Tom Swift," replied our hero, and again he wished he had not told. This time he was sure the tramp started and glanced at him quickly, but perhaps it was only his imagination.

"Tom Swift," repeated the man musingly, and his tones were different from the whining ones in which he had asked for money. Then, as if recollecting the part he was playing, he added: "I s'pose dey calls youse dat because youse rides so quick on dat machine. But I'm certainly obliged to youse—Tom Swift, an' I hopes youse gits t' Albany, in Jersey, in good time."

He turned away, and Tom was beginning to breathe more easily when the ragged man, with a quick gesture, reached out and grabbed hold of the motor-cycle. He gave it such a pull that it was nearly torn from Tom's grasp. The lad was so startled at the sudden exhibition of vindictiveness on the part of the tramp that he did not know what to do. Then, before he could recover himself, the tramp darted into the bushes.

"I guess Happy Harry—dat's me—has spoiled your ride t' Albany!" the tramp cried. "Maybe next time youse won't run down poor fellers on de road," and with that, the ragged man, shaking his fist at Tom, was lost to sight in the underbrush.

"Well, if that isn't a queer end up," mused Tom. "He must be crazy. I hope I don't meet you again, Happy Harry, or whatever your name is. Guess I'll get out of this neighborhood."

CHAPTER XII

THE MEN IN THE AUTO

Tom first made sure that the package containing the model was still safely in place back of his saddle on the motor-cycle. Finding it there he next put his hand in his pocket to see that he had the papers.

"They're all right," spoke Tom aloud. "I didn't know but what that chap might have worked a pickpocket game on me. I'm glad I didn't meet him after dark. Well, it's a good thing it's no worse. I wonder if he tried to get my machine away from me? Don't believe he'd know how to ride it if he did."

Tom wheeled his motor-cycle to a hard side-path along the old road, and jumped into the saddle. He worked the pedals preparatory to turning on the gasolene and spark to set the motor in motion. As he threw forward the levers, having acquired what he thought was the necessary momentum, he was surprised that no explosion followed. The motor seemed "dead."

"That's queer," he thought, and he began to pedal more rapidly. "It always used to start easily. "Maybe it doesn't like this sandy road."

It was hard work sending the heavy machine along by "leg power," and once more, when he had acquired what he thought was sufficient speed, Tom turned on the power. But no explosions followed, and in some alarm he jumped to the ground.

"Something's wrong," he said aloud. "That tramp must have damaged the machine when he yanked it so." Tom went quickly over the different parts. It did not take him long to discover what the trouble was. One of the wires, leading from the batteries to the motor, which wire served to carry the current of electricity that exploded the mixture of air and gasolene, was missing. It had been broken off close to the battery box and the spark plug.

"That's what Happy Harry did!" exclaimed Tom. "He pulled that wire off when he yanked my machine. That's what he meant by hoping I'd get to Albany. That fellow was no tramp' He was disguised, and up to some game. And he knows something about motor-cycles, too, or he never would have taken that wire. I'm stalled, now, for I haven't got another piece. I ought to have brought some. I'll have to push this machine until I get to town, or else go back home."

The young inventor looked up and down the lonely road, undecided what to do. To return home meant that he would be delayed in getting to Albany, for he would lose a day. If he pushed on to Pompville he might be able to get a bit of wire there.

Tom decided that was his best plan, and plodded on through the thick sand. He had not gone more than a quarter of a mile, every step seeming harder than the preceding one, when he heard, from the woods close at his left hand, a gun fired. He jumped so that he nearly let the motor-cycle fall over, for a wild idea came into his head that the tramp had shot at him. With a quickly-beating heart the lad looked about him.

"I wonder if that was Happy Harry?" he mused.

There was a crackling in the bushes and Tom, wondering what he might do to protect himself, looked toward the place whence the noise proceeded. A moment later a hunter stepped into view. The man carried a gun and wore a canvas suit, a belt about his waist being filled with cartridges.

"Hello!" he exclaimed pleasantly. Then, seeing a look of alarm on the lad's face, he went on:

"I hope I didn't shoot in your direction, young man; did I?"

"No—no, sir," replied the youthful inventor, who had hardly recovered his composure. "I heard your gun, and I imagined——"

"Did you think you had been shot? You must have a very vivid imagination, for I fired in the air."

"No, I didn't exactly think that," replied Tom, "but I just had an encounter with an ugly tramp, and I feared he might be using me for a target."

"Is that so. I hadn't noticed any tramps around here, and I've been in these woods nearly all day. Did he harm you?"

"No, not me, but my motor-cycle," and the lad explained.

"Pshaw! That's too bad!" exclaimed the hunter. "I wish I could supply you with a bit of wire, but I haven't any. I'm just walking about, trying my new gun."

"I shouldn't think you'd find anything to shoot this time of year," remarked Tom.

"I don't expect to," answered the hunter, who had introduced himself as Theodore Duncan. "But I have just purchased a new gun, and I wanted to try it. I expect to do considerable hunting this fall, and so I'm getting ready for it."

"Do you live near here?"

"Well, about ten miles away, on the other side of Lake Carlopa, but I am fond of long walks in the woods. If you ever get to Waterford I wish you'd come and see me, Mr. Swift. I have heard of your father."

"I will, Mr. Duncan; but if I don't get something to repair my machine with I'm not likely to get anywhere right away."

"Well, I wish I could help you, but I haven't the least ingenuity when it comes to machinery. Now if I could help you track down that tramp——"

"Oh, no, thank you, I'd rather not have anything more to do with him."

"If I caught sight of him now," resumed the hunter, "I fancy I could make him halt, and, perhaps, give you back the wire. I'm a pretty good shot, even if this is a new gun. I've been practicing at improvised targets all day."

"No; the less I have to do with him, the better I shall like it," answered Tom, "though I'm much obliged to you. I'll manage somehow until I get to Pompville."

He started off again, the hunter disappearing in the woods, whence the sound of his gun was again heard.

"He's a queer chap," murmured Tom, "but I

like him. Perhaps I may see him when I go to Waterford, if I ever do."

Tom was destined to see the hunter again, at no distant time, and under strange circumstances. But now the lad's whole attention was taken up with the difficulty in which he found himself. Vainly musing on what object the tramp could have had in breaking off the wire, the young inventor trudged on.

"I guess he was one of the gang after dad's invention," thought Tom, "and he must have wanted to hinder me from getting to Albany, though why I can't imagine." With a dubious shake of his head Tom proceeded. It was hard work pushing the heavy machine through the sand, and he was puffing before he had gone very far.

"I certainly am up against it," he murmured. "But if I can get a bit of wire in Pompville I'll be all right. If I can't——"

Just then Tom saw something which caused him to utter an exclamation of delight.

"That's the very thing!" he cried. "Why didn't I think of it before?"

Leaving his motor-cycle standing against a tree Tom hurried to a fence that separated the road from a field. The fence was a barbed-wire one, and in a moment Tom had found a broken strand.

"Guess no one will care if I take a piece of this," he reasoned. "It will answer until I can get more. I'll have it in place in a jiffy!"

It did not take long to get his pliers from his toolbag and snip off a piece of the wire. Untwisting it he took out the sharp barbs, and then was ready to attach it to the binding posts of the battery box and the spark plug.

"Hold on, though!" he exclaimed as he paused in the work. "It's got to be insulated, or it will vibrate against the metal of the machine and short circuit. I have it! My handkerchief! I s'pose Mrs. Baggert will kick at tearing up a good one, but I can't help it."

Tom took a spare handkerchief from the bundle in which he had a few belongings carried with the idea of spending the night at an Albany hotel, and he was soon wrapping strips of linen around the wire, tying them with pieces of string.

"There!" he exclaimed at length. "That's insulated good enough, I guess. Now to fasten it on and start."

The young inventor, who was quick with tools, soon had the improvised wire in place. He tested the spark and found that it was almost as good as when the regular copper conductor was in place. Then, having taken a spare bit of the barbed-wire along in case of another emergency, he jumped on the motor-cycle, pedaled it until sufficient speed was attained, and turned on the power.

"That's the stuff!" he cried as the welcome explosions sounded. "I guess I've fooled Happy Harry! I'll get to Albany pretty nearly on time, anyhow. But that tramp surely had me worried for a while."

He rode into Pompville, and on inquiring in a plumbing shop managed to get a bit of copper wire that answered better than did the galvanized piece from the fence. The readjustment was quickly made, and he was on his way again. As it was getting close to noon he stopped near a little spring outside of Pompville and ate a sandwich, washing it down with the cold water. Then he started for Centreford.

As he was coming into the city he heard an automobile behind him. He steered to one side of the road to give the big car plenty of room to pass, but it did not come on as speedily as he thought it would. He looked back and saw that it was going to stop near him. Accordingly he shut off the power of his machine.

"Is this the road to Centreford?" asked one of the travelers in the auto.

"Straight ahead," answered the lad.

At the sound of his voice one of the men in

the big touring car leaned forward and whispered something to one on the front seat. The second man nodded, and looked closely at Tom. The youth, in turn, stared at the men. He could not distinguish their faces, as they had on auto goggles.

"How many miles is it?" asked the man who had whispered, and at the sound of his voice Tom felt a vague sense that he had heard it before.

"Three," answered the young inventor, and once more he saw the men whisper among themselves.

"Thanks," spoke the driver of the car, and he threw in the gears. As the big machine darted ahead the goggles which one of the men wore slipped off. Tom had a glimpse of his face.

"Anson Morse!" he exclaimed. "If that isn't the man who was sneaking around dad's motor shop he's his twin brother! I wonder if those aren't the men who are after the patent model? I must be on my guard!" and Tom, watching the car fade out of sight on the road ahead of him, slowly started his motor-cycle He was much puzzled and alarmed.

CHAPTER XIII

CAUGHT IN A STORM

THE more Tom tried to reason out the cause of the men's actions, the more he dwelt upon his encounter with the tramp, and the harder he endeavored to seek a solution of the queer puzzle, the more complicated it seemed. He rode on until he saw in a valley below him the buildings of the town of Centreford, and, with a view of them, a new idea came into his mind.

"I'll go get a good dinner," he decided, "and perhaps that will help me to think more clearly. That's what dad always does when he's puzzling over an invention." He was soon seated in a restaurant, where he ate a substantial dinner. "I'm just going to stop puzzling over this matter," he decided. "I'll push on to Albany and tell the lawyer, Mr. Crawford. Perhaps he can advise me."

Once this decision was made Tom felt better.

"That's just what I needed," he thought; "some

one to shift the responsibility upon. I'll let the lawyers do the worrying. That's what they're paid for. Now for Albany, and I hope I don't have to stop, except for supper, until I get there. I've got to do some night riding, but I've got a powerful lamp, and the roads from now on are good."

Tom was soon on his way again. The highway leading to Albany was a hard, macadam one, and he fairly flew along the level stretches.

"This is making good time," he thought. "I won't be so very late, after all; that is, if nothing delays me."

The young inventor looked up into the sky. The sun, which had been shining brightly all day, was now hidden behind a mass of hazy clouds, for which the rider was duly grateful, as it was becoming quite warm.

"It's more like summer than I thought," said Tom to himself. "I shouldn't be surprised if we got rain to-morrow."

Another look at the sky confirmed him in this belief, and he had not gone on many miles farther when his opinion was suddenly changed. This was brought about by a dull rumble in the west, and Tom noticed that a bank of low-lying clouds had formed, the black, inky masses of vapor being whirled upward as if by some powerful blast.

"Guess my storm is going to arrive ahead of time," he said. "I'd better look for shelter."

With a suddenness that characterizes summer showers, the whole sky became overcast. The thunder increased, and the flashes of lightning became more frequent and dazzling. A wind sprang up and blew clouds of dust in Tom's face.

"It certainly is going to be a thunder storm," he admitted. "I'm bound to be delayed now, for the roads will be mucky. Well, there's no help for it. If I get to Albany before midnight I'll be doing well."

A few drops of rain splashed on his hands, and as he looked up to note the state of the sky others fell in his face. They were big drops, and where they splashed on the road they formed little globules of mud.

"I'll head for that big tree," thought Tom. "It will give me some shelter. I'll wait there——"
His words were interrupted by a deafening crash of thunder which followed close after a blinding flash. "No tree for mine!" murmured Tom. "I forgot that they're dangerous in a storm. I wonder where I can stay?"

He turned on all the power possible and sprinted ahead. Around a curve in the road he went, leaning over to preserve his balance, and just as the rain came pelting down in a torrent he saw

just ahead of him a white church on the lonely
country road. To one side was a long shed, where
the farmers were in the habit of leaving their
teams when they came to service.

"Just the thing!" cried the boy; "and just in
time!"

He turned his motor-cycle into the yard surrounding the church, and a moment later had
come to a stop beneath the shed. It was broad
and long, furnishing a good protection against the
storm, which had now burst in all its fury.

Tom was not very wet, and looking to see that
the model, which was partly of wood, had suf-
fered no damage, the lad gave his attention to his
machine.

"Seems to be all right," he murmured. "I'll
just oil her up while I'm waiting. This can't last
long; it's raining too hard."

He busied himself over the motor-cycle, adjusting a nut that had been rattled loose, and
putting some oil on the bearings. The rain kept
up steadily, and when he had completed his at-
tentions to his machine Tom looked out from
under the protection of the shed.

"It certainly is coming down for keeps," he
murmured. "This trip is a regular hoodoo so
far. Hope I have it better coming back."

As he looked down the road he espied an automobile coming through the mist of rain. It was an open car, and as he saw the three men in it huddled up under the insufficient protection of some blankets, Tom said:

"They'd ought to come in here. There's lots of room. Maybe they don't see it. I'll call to them."

The car was almost opposite the shed which was close to the roadside. Tom was about to call when one of the men in the auto looked up. He saw the shelter and spoke to the chauffeur. The latter was preparing to steer up into the shed when the two men on the rear seat caught sight of Tom.

"Why, that's the same car that passed me a while ago," said the young inventor half aloud. "The one that contained those men whom I suspected might be after dad's patent. I hope they——"

He did not finish his sentence, for at that instant the chauffeur quickly swung the machine around and headed it back into the road. Clearly the men were not going to take advantage of the shelter of the shed.

"That's mighty strange," murmured Tom. "They certainly saw me, and as soon as they did they turned away. Can they be afraid of me?"

He went to the edge of the shelter and peered

out. The auto had disappeared down the road behind a veil of rain, and, shaking his head over the strange occurrence, Tom went back to where he had left his motor-cycle.

"Things are getting more and more muddled," he said. "I'm sure those were the same men, and yet——"

He shrugged his shoulders. The puzzle was getting beyond him.

CHAPTER XIV

ATTACKED FROM BEHIND

STEADILY the rain came down, the wind driving it under the shed until Tom was hard put to
find a place where the drops would not reach him.
He withdrew into a far corner, taking his motor-
cycle with him, and then, sitting on a block of
wood, under the rough mangers where the horses
were fed while the farmers attended church, the
lad thought over the situation. He could make
little of it, and the more he tried the worse it
seemed to become. He looked out across the wet
landscape.

"I wonder if this is ever going to stop?" he
mused. "It looks as if it was in for an all-day
pour, yet we ought only to have a summer shower.
by rights.

"But then I guess what I think about it won't
influence the weather man a bit. I might as well
make myself comfortable, for I can't do anything.
Let's see. If I get to Fordham by six o'clock

I ought to be able to make Albany by nine, as it's only forty miles. I'll get supper in Fordham, and push on. That is, I will if the rain stops."

That was the most necessary matter to have happen first, and Tom arising from his seat strolled over to the front of the shed to look out.

"I believe it is getting lighter in the west," he told himself. "Yes, the clouds are lifting. It's going to clear. It's only a summer shower, after all."

But just as he said that there came a sudden squall of wind and rain, fiercer than any which had preceded. Tom was driven back to his seat on the log. It was quite chilly now, and he noticed that near where he sat there was a big opening in the rear of the shed, where a couple of boards were off.

"This must be a draughty place in winter," he observed. "If I could find a drier spot I'd sit there, but this seems to be the best," and he remained there, musing on many things. Suddenly in the midst of his thoughts he imagined he heard the sound of an automobile approaching. "I wonder if those men are coming back here?" he exclaimed. "If they are——"

The youth again arose, and went to the front of the shed. He could see nothing, and came back to escape the rain. There was no doubt but that the shower would soon be over, and looking at his watch, Tom began to calculate when he might arrive in Albany.

He was busy trying to figure out the best plan to pursue, and was hardly conscious of his surroundings. Seated on the log, with his back to the opening in the shed, the young inventor could not see a figure stealthily creeping up through the wet grass. Nor could he see an automobile, which had come to a stop back of the horse shelter—an automobile containing two rain-soaked men, who were anxiously watching the one stealing through the grass.

Tom put his watch back into his pocket and looked out into the storm. It was almost over. The sun was trying to shine through the clouds, and only a few drops were falling. The youth stretched with a yawn, for he was tired of sitting still. At the moment when he raised his arms to relieve his muscles something was thrust through the opening behind him. It was a long club, and an instant later it descended on the lad's head. He went down in a heap, limp and motionless.

Through the opening leaped a man. He bent over Tom, looked anxiously at him, and then, stepping to the place where the boards were off the shed, he motioned to the men in the automobile. They hurried from the machine, and were soon beside their companion.

"I knocked him out, all right," observed the man who had reached through and dealt Tom the blow with the club.

"Knocked him out! I should say you did, Featherton!" exclaimed one who appeared better dressed than the others. "Have you killed him?"

"No; but I wish you wouldn't mention my name, Mr. Appleson. I—I don't like——"

"Nonsense, Featherton. No one can hear us. But I'm afraid you've done for the chap. I didn't want him harmed."

"Oh, I guess Featherton knows how to do it, Appleson," commented the third man. "He's had experience that way, eh, Featherton?"

"Yes, Mr. Morse; but if you please I wish you wouldn't mention——"

"All right, Featherton, I know what you mean," rejoined the man addressed as Morse. "Now let's see if we have drawn a blank or not. I think he has with him the very thing we want."

"Doesn't seem to be about his person," observed Appleson, as he carefully felt about the clothing of the unfortunate Tom.

"Very likely not. It's too bulky. But there's his motor-cycle over there. It looks as if what we wanted was on the back of the saddle. Jove, Featherton, but I think he's coming to!"

Tom stirred uneasily and moved his arms, while a moan came from between his parted lips.

"I've got some stuff that will fix him!" exclaimed the man addressed as Featherton, and who had been operating the automobile. He took something from his pocket and leaned over Tom. In a moment the young inventor was still again.

"Quick now, see if it's there," directed Morse, and Appleson hurried over to the machine.

"Here it is!" he called. "I'll take it to our car, and we can get away."

"Are you going to leave him here like this?" asked Morse.

"Yes; why not?"

"Because some one might have seen him come in here, and also remember that we, too, came in this direction."

"What would you do?"

"Take him down the road a way and leave him. We can find some shed near a farmhouse where he and his machine will be out of sight until we get far enough away. Besides, I don't like to leave him so far from help, unconscious as he is."

"Oh, you're getting chicken-hearted," said Appleson with a sneer. "However, have your way about it. I wonder what has become of Jake Burke? He was to meet us in Centreford, but he did not show up."

"Oh, I shouldn't be surprised if he had trouble in that tramp rig he insisted on adopting. I told him he was running a risk, but he said he had masqueraded as a tramp before."

"So he has. He's pretty good at it. Now, Simpson, if you will——"

"Not Simpson! I thought you agreed to call me Featherton," interrupted the chauffeur, turning to Morse and Appleson.

"Oh, so we did. I forgot that this lad met us one day, and heard me call you Simpson," admitted Morse. "Well, Featherton it shall be. But we haven't much time. It's stopped raining, and the roads will soon be well traveled. We must get away, and if we are to take the lad and his machine to some secluded place, we'd better be at it. No use waiting for Burke. He can look out after himself. Anyhow, we have the model now, and there's no use in him hanging around Swift's shop, as he intended to do, waiting for a chance to sneak in after it. Appleson, if you and Simpson—I mean Featherton—will carry young Swift, I'll shove his wheel along to the auto, and we can put it and him in."

The two men, first looking through the hole

in the shed to make sure they were not observed, went out, carrying Tom, who was no light load. Morse followed them, pushing the motor-cycle, and carrying under one arm the bundle containing the valuable model, which he had detached.

"I think this is the time we get ahead of Mr. Swift," murmured Morse, pulling his black mustache, when he and his companions had reached the car in the field. "We have just what we want now."

"Yes, but we had hard enough work getting it," observed Appleson. "Only by luck we saw this lad come in here, or we would have had to chase all over for him, and maybe then we would have missed him. Hurry, Simpson—I mean Featherton. It's getting late, and we've got lots to do."

The chauffeur sprang to his seat, Appleson taking his place beside him. The motor-cycle was tied on behind the big touring car, and with the unconscious form of Tom in the tonneau, beside Morse, who stroked his mustache nervously, the auto started off. The storm had passed, and the sun was shining brightly, but Tom could not see it.

CHAPTER XV

A VAIN SEARCH

SEVERAL hours later Tom had a curious dream. He imagined he was wandering about in the polar regions, and that it was very cold. He was trying to reason with himself that he could not possibly be on an expedition searching for the North Pole, still he felt such a keen wind blowing over his scantily-covered body that he shivered. He shivered so hard, in fact, that he shivered himself awake, and when he tried to pierce the darkness that enveloped him he was startled, for a moment, with the idea that perhaps, after all, he had wandered off to some unknown country.

For it was quite dark and cold. He was in a daze, and there was a curious smell about him —an odor that he tried to recall. Then, all at once, it came to him what it was—chloroform Once his father had undergone an operation, and to deaden his pain chloroform had been used.

"I've been chloroformed!" exclaimed the young inventor, and his words sounded strange in his ears. "That's it. I've met with an accident—riding my motor-cycle. I must have hit my head, for it hurts fearful. They picked me up, carried me to a hospital and have operated on me. I vonder if they took off an arm or leg? I wonder what hospital I'm in? Why is it so dark and cold?"

As he asked himself these questions his brain gradually cleared from the haze caused by the cowardly blow, and from the chloroform that had been administered by Featherton.

Tom's first act was to feel first of one arm, then the other. Having satisfied himself that neither of these members were mutilated he reached down to his legs.

"Why, they're all right, too," he murmured. "I wonder what they did to me? That's certainly chloroform I smell, and my head feels as if some one had sat on it. I wonder——"

Quickly he put up his hands to his head. There appeared to be nothing the matter with it, save that there was quite a lump on the back, where the club had struck.

"I seem to be all here," went on Tom, much mystified. "But where am I? That's the question. It's a funny hospital, so cold and dark——"

Just then his hands came in contact with the cold ground on which he was lying.

"Why, I'm outdoors!" he exclaimed. Then in a flash it all came back to him—how he had gone to wait under the church shed until the rain was over.

"I fell asleep, and now it's night," the youth went on. "No wonder I am sore and stiff. And that chloroform——" He could not account for that, and he paused, puzzled once more. Then he struggled to a sitting position. His head was strangely dizzy, but he persisted, and got to his feet. He could see nothing, and groped around in the dark, until he thought to strike a match. Fortunately he had a number in his pocket. As the little flame flared up Tom started in surprise.

"This isn't the church shed!" he exclaimed. It's much smaller! I'm in a different place! Great Scott! but what has happened to me?"

The match burned Tom's fingers and he dropped it. The darkness closed in once more, but Tom was used to it by this time, and looking ahead of him he could make out that the shed was an open one, similar to the one where he had taken shelter. He could see the sky studded with stars, and could feel the cold night wind blowing in.

"My motor-cycle!" he exclaimed in alarm. "The model of dad's invention—the papers!"

Our hero thrust his hand into his pocket. The

papers were gone! Hurriedly he lighted another match. It took but an instant to glance rapidly about the small shed. His machine was not in sight!

Tom felt his heart sink. After all his precautions he had been robbed. The precious model was gone, and it had been his proposition to take it to Albany in this manner. What would his father say?

The lad lighted match after match, and made a rapid tour of the shed. The motor-cycle was not to be seen. But what puzzled Tom more than anything else was how he had been brought from the church shed to the one where he had awakened from his stupor.

"Let me try to think," said the boy, speaking aloud, for it seemed to help him. "The last I remember is seeing that automobile, with those mysterious men in, approaching. Then it disappeared in the rain. I thought I heard it again, but I couldn't see it. I was sitting on the log, and—and—well, that's all I can remember. I wonder if those men——"

The young inventor paused. Like a flash it came to him that the men were responsible for his predicament. They had somehow made him insensible, stolen his motor-cycle, the papers and the model, and then brought him to this place, wherever it was. Tom was a shrewd reasoner, and he soon evolved a theory which he afterward learned was the correct one. He reasoned out almost every step in the crime of which he was the victim, and at last came to the conclusion that the men had stolen up behind the shed and attacked him.

"Now, the next question to settle," spoke Tom, "is to learn where I am. How far did those scoundrels carry me, and what has become of my motor-cycle?"

He walked toward the point of the shed where he could observe the stars gleaming, and there he lighted some more matches, hoping he might see his machine. By the gleam of the little flame he noted that he was in a farmyard, and he was just puzzling his brain over the question as to what city or town he might be near when he heard a voice shouting:

"Here, what you lightin' them matches for? You want to set the place afire? Who be you, anyhow—a tramp?"

It was unmistakably the voice of a farmer, and Tom could hear footsteps approaching on the run.

"Who be you, anyhow?" the voice repeated. "I'll have the constable after you in a jiffy if you're a tramp."

"I'm not a tramp," called Tom promptly. "I've met with an accident. Where am I?"

"Humph! Mighty funny if you don't know where you are," commented the farmer. "Jed, bring a lantern until I take a look at who this is."

"All right, pop," answered another voice, and a moment later Tom saw a tall man standing in front of him.

"I'll give you a look at me without waiting for the lantern," said Tom quickly, and he struck a match, holding it so that the gleam fell upon his face.

"Salt mackerel! It's a young feller!" exclaimed the farmer. "Who be you, anyhow, and what you doin' here?"

"That's just what I would like to know," said Tom, passing his hand over his head, which was still paining him. "Am I near Albany? That's where I started for this morning."

"Albany? You're a good way from Albany," replied the farmer. "You're in the village of Dunkirk."

"How far is that from Centreford?"

"About seventy miles."

"As far as that?" cried Tom. "They must have carried me a good way in their automobile."

"Was you in that automobile?" demanded the farmer.

"Which one?" asked Tom quickly.

"The one that stopped down the road just before supper. I see it, but I didn't pay no attention to it. If I'd 'a' knowed you fell out, though, I'd 'a' come to help you."

"I didn't fall out, Mr.—er——" Tom paused.

"Blackford is my name; Amos Blackford."

"Well, Mr. Blackford, I didn't fall out. I was drugged and brought here."

"Drugged! Salt mackerel! But there's been a crime committed, then. Jed, hurry up with that lantern an' git your deputy sheriff's badge on. There's been druggin' an' all sorts of crimes committed. I've caught one of the victims. Hurry up! My son's a deputy sheriff," he added, by way of an explanation.

"Then I hope he can help me catch the scoundrels who robbed me," said Tom.

"Robbed you, did they? Hurry up, Jed. There's been a robbery! We'll rouse the neighborhood an' search for the villains. Hurry up, Jed!"

"I'd rather find my motor-cycle, and a valuable model which was on it, than locate those men," went on Tom. "They also took some papers from me."

Then he told how he had started for Albany, adding his theory of how he had been attacked and carried away in the auto. The latter part of it was borne out by the testimony of Mr. Blackford.

"What I know about it," said the farmer, when his son Jed had arrived on the scene with a lantern and his badge, "is that jest about supper time I saw an automobile stop down the road a bit. It was gittin' dusk, an' I saw some men git out. I didn't pay no attention to them, 'cause I was busy about the milkin'. The next I knowed I seen some one strikin' matches in my wagon shed, an' I come out to see what it was."

"The men must have brought me all the way from the church shed near Centreford to here," declared Tom. "Then they lifted me out and put me in your shed. Maybe they left my motorcycle also."

"I didn't see nothin' like that," said the farmer. "Is that what you call one of them two-wheeled lickity-split things that a man sits on the middle of an' goes like chain-lightning?"

"It is," said Tom. "I wish you'd help me look for it."

The farmer and his son agreed, and other lanterns having been secured, a search was made. After about half an hour the motor-cycle was discovered in some bushes at the side of the road, near where the automobile had stopped. But the model was missing from it, and a careful search near where the machine had been hidden did not reveal it. Nor did as careful a hunt as they could make in the darkness disclose any clues to the scoundrels who had drugged and robbed Tom.

CHAPTER XVI

BACK HOME

"WE'VE got to organize a regular searchin'
party," declared Jed Blackford, after he and his
father, together with Tom and the farmer's hired
man, had searched up and down the road by the
light of lanterns. "We'll organize a posse an'
have a regular hunt. This is the worst crime
that's been committed in this deestrict in many
years, an' I'm goin' to run the scoundrels to
earth."

"Don't be talkin' nonsense, Jed," interrupted his
father. "You won't catch them fellers in a hundred years. They're miles an' miles away from
here by this time in their automobile. All you can
do is to notify the sheriff. I guess we'd better
give this young man some attention. Let's see,
you said your name was Quick, didn't you?"

"No, but it's very similar," answered Tom with
a smile. "It's Swift."

"I knowed it was something had to do with

speed," went on Mr. Blackford. "Wa'al, now, s'pose you come in the house an' have a hot cup of tea. You look sort of draggled out."

Tom was glad enough to avail himself of the kind invitation, and he was soon in the comfortable kitchen, relating his story, with more detail, to the farmer and his family. Mrs. Blackford applied some home-made remedies to the lump on the youth's head, and it felt much better.

"I'd like to take a look at my motor-cycle," he said, after his second cup of tea. "I want to see if those men damaged it any. If they have I'm going to have trouble getting back home to tell my father of my bad luck. Poor dad! He will be very much worried when I tell him the model and his patent papers have been stolen."

"It's too bad!" exclaimed Mrs. Blackford. "I wish I had hold of them scoundrels!" and her usually gentle face bore a severe frown. "Of course you can have your thing-a-ma-bob in to see if it's hurt, but please don't start it in here. They make a terrible racket."

"No, I'll look it over in the woodshed," promised Tom. "If it's all right I think I'll start back home at once."

"No, you can't do that," declared Mr. Blackford. "You're in no condition to travel. You might fall off an' git hurt. It's nearly ten o'clock now. You jest stay here all night, an' in the mornin', if you feel all right, you can start off. I couldn't let you go to-night."

Indeed, Tom did not feel very much like undertaking the journey, for the blow on his head had made him dazed, and the chloroform caused a sick feeling. Mr. Blackford wheeled the motorcycle into the woodhouse, which opened from the kitchen, and there the youth went over the machine. He was glad to find that it had sustained no damage. In the meanwhile Jed had gone off to tell the startling news to near-by farmers. Quite a throng, with lanterns, went up and down the road, but all the evidence they could find were the marks of the automobile wheels, which clues were not very satisfactory.

"But we'll catch them in the mornin'," declared the deputy sheriff. "I'll know that automobile again if I see it. It was painted red."

"That's the color of a number of automobiles," said Tom with a smile. "I'm afraid you'll have trouble identifying it by that means. I am surprised, though, that they did not carry my motorcycle away with them. It is a valuable machine."

"They were afraid to," declared Jed. "It would look queer to see a machine like that in an auto. Of course when they were going along country roads in the evening it didn't much matter, but when they headed for the city, as they probably did, they knew it would attract suspicion to 'em. I know, for I've been a deputy sheriff 'most a year."

"I believe you're right," agreed Tom. "They didn't dare take the motor-cycle with them, but they hid it, hoping I would not find it. I'd rather have the model and the papers, though, than half a dozen motor-cycles."

"Maybe the police will help you find them," said Mrs. Blackford. "Jed, you must telephone to the police the first thing in the morning. It's a shame the way criminals are allowed to go on. If honest people did those things, they'd be arrested in a minute, but it seems that scoundrels can do as they please."

"You wait; I'll catch 'em!" declared Jed confidently. "I'll organize another posse in the mornin'."

"Well, I know one thing, and that is that the place for this young man is in bed!" exclaimed motherly Mrs. Blackford, and she insisted on Tom retiring. He was somewhat restless at first, and the thought of the loss of the model and the papers preyed on his mind. Then, utterly exhausted, he sank into a heavy slumber, and did not awaken until the sun was shining in his window the next morning. A good breakfast made

him feel somewhat better, and he was more like
the resourceful Tom Swift of old when he went
to get his motor-cycle in shape for the ride back
to Shopton.

"Well, I hope you find those criminals," said
Mr. Blackford, as he watched Tom oiling the
machine. "If you're ever out this way again, stop
off and see us."

"Yes, do," urged Mrs. Blackford, who was
getting ready to churn. Her husband looked at
the old-fashioned barrel and dasher arrangement,
which she was filling with cream.

"What's the matter with the new churn?" he
asked in some surprise.

"It's broken," she replied. "It's always the way
with those new-fangled things. It works ever so
much nicer than this old one, though," she went
on to Tom, "but it gets out of order easy."

"Let me look at it," suggested the young inventor. "I know something about machinery."

The churn, which worked by a system of cogs
and a handle, was brought from the woodshed.
Tom soon saw what the trouble was. One of the
cogs had become displaced. It did not take him
five minutes, with the tools he carried on his
motor-cycle, to put it back, and the churn was
ready to use.

"Well, I declare!" exclaimed Mrs. Blackford. "You are handy at such things!"

"Oh, it's just a knack," replied Tom modestly. "Now I'll put a plug in there, and the cog wheel won't come loose again. The manufacturers of it ought to have done that. I imagine lots of people have this same trouble with these churns."

"Indeed they do," asserted Mrs. Blackford. "Sallie Armstrong has one, and it got out of order the first week they had it. I'll let her look at mine, and maybe her husband can fix it."

"I'd go and do it myself, but I want to get home," said Tom, and then he showed her how, by inserting a small iron plug in a certain place, there would be no danger of the cog coming loose again.

"That's certainly slick!" exclaimed Mr. Blackford. "Well, I wish you good luck, Mr. Swift, and if I see those scoundrels around this neighborhood again I'll make 'em wish they'd let you alone."

"That's what," added Jed, polishing his badge with his big, red handkerchief.

Mrs. Blackford transferred the cream to the new churn which Tom had fixed, and as he rode off down the highway on his motor-cycle, she waved one hand to him, while with the other she operated the handle of the apparatus.

"Now for a quick run to Shopton to tell dad the bad news," spoke Tom to himself as he turned on full speed and dashed away. "My trip has been a failure so far."

CHAPTER XVII

MR. SWIFT IN DESPAIR

TOM was thinking of many things as his speedy machine carried him mile after mile nearer home. By noon he was over half way on his journey, and he stopped in a small village for his dinner.

"I think I'll make inquiries of the police here, to see if they caught sight of those men," decided Tom as he left the restaurant. "Though I am inclined to believe they kept on to Albany, or some large city, where they have their headquarters. They will want to make use of dad's model as soon as possible, though what they will do with it I don't know." He tried to telephone to his father, but could get no connection, as the wire was being repaired.

The police force of the place where Tom had stopped for lunch was like the town itself—small and not of much consequence. The chief constable, for he was not what one could call a chief of police, had heard of the matter from the alarm sent out in all directions from Dunkirk, where Mr. Blackford lived.

"You don't mean to tell me you're the young man who was chloroformed and robbed!" exclaimed the constable, looking at Tom as if he doubted his word.

"I'm the young man," declared our hero. "Have you seen anything of the thieves?"

"Not a thing, though I've instructed all my men to keep a sharp lookout for a red automobile, with three scoundrels in it. My men are to make an arrest on sight."

"How many men have you?"

"Two," was the rather surprising answer; "but one has to work on a farm daytimes, so I ain't really got but one in what you might call active service."

Tom restrained a desire to laugh. At any rate, the aged constable meant well.

"One of my men seen a red automobile, a little while before you come in my office," went on the official, "but it wasn't the one wanted, 'cause a young woman was running it all alone. It struck me as rather curious that a woman would trust herself all alone in one of them things; wouldn't it you?"

"Oh, no, women and young ladies often operate them," said Tom.

"I should think you'd find one handier than the two-wheeled apparatus you have out there," went on the constable, indicating the motor-cycle, which Tom had stood up against a tree.

"I may have one some day," replied the young inventor. "But I guess I'll be moving on now. Here's my address, in case you hear anything of those men, but I don't imagine you will."

"Me either. Fellows as slick as them are won't come back this way and run the chance of being arrested by my men. I have two on duty nights," he went on proudly, "besides myself, so you see we're pretty well protected."

Tom thanked him for the trouble he had taken, and was soon on his way again. He swept on along the quiet country roads anxious for the time when he could consult with his father over what would be the best course to take.

When Tom was about a mile away from his house he saw in the road ahead of him a rickety old wagon, and a second glance at it told him the outfit belonged to Eradicate Sampson, for the animal drawing the vehicle was none other than the mule, Boomerang.

"But what in the world is Rad up to?" mused Tom, for the colored man was out of the wagon and was going up and down in the grass at the side of the highway in a curious fashion. "I guess he's lost something," decided Tom.

When he got nearer he saw what Eradicate was doing. The colored man was pushing a lawn-mower slowly to and fro in the tall, rank grass that grew beside the thoroughfare, and at the sound of Tom's motor-cycle the negro looked up. There was such a woe-begone expression on his face that Tom at once stopped his machine and got off.

"What's the matter, Rad?" Tom asked.

"Mattah, Mistah Swift? Why, dere's a pow'-ful lot de mattah, an' dat's de truff. I'se been swindled, dat's what I has."

"Swindled? How?"

"Well, it's dis-a-way. Yo' see dis yeah lawn-moah?"

"Yes; it doesn't seem to work," and Tom glanced critically at it. As Eradicate pushed it slowly to and fro, the blades did not revolve, and the wheels slipped along on the grass.

"No, sah, it doan't work, an' dat's how I've been swindled, Mistah Swift. Yo' see, I done traded mah ole grindstone off for dis yeah lawn-moah, an' I got stuck."

"What, that old grindstone that was broken in two, and that you fastened together with con-crete?" asked Tom, for he had seen the outfit with which Eradicate, in spare times between cleaning and whitewashing, had gone about the country, sharpening knives and scissors. "You don't mean that old, broken one?"

"Dat's what I mean, Mistah Swift. Why, it was all right. I mended it so dat de break wouldn't show, an' it would sharpen things if yo' run it slow. But dis yeah lawn-moah won't wuk slow ner fast."

"I guess it was an even exchange, then," went on Tom. "You didn't get bitten any worse than the other fellow did."

"Yo' doan't s'pose yo' kin fix dis yeah moah so's I kin use it, does yo', Mistah Swift?" asked Eradicate, not bothering to go into the ethics of the matter. "I reckon now with summah comin' on I kin make mo' with a lawn-moah than I kin with a grindstone—dat is, ef I kin git it to wuk. I jest got it a while ago an' decided to try it, but it won't cut no grass."

"I haven't much time," said Tom, "for I'm anxious to get home, but I'll take a look at it."

Tom leaned his motor-cycle against the fence. He could no more pass a bit of broken machinery, which he thought he could mend, than some men and boys can pass by a baseball game without stopping to watch it, no matter how pressed they are for time. It was Tom's hobby, and he delighted in nothing so much as tinkering with machines, from lawn-mowers to steam engines.

Tom took hold of the handle, which Eradicate gladly relinquished to him, and his trained touch told him at once what was the trouble.

"Some one has had the wheels off and put them on wrong, Rad," he said. "The ratchet and pawl are reversed. This mower would work backwards, if that were possible."

"Am dat so, Mistah Swift?"

"That's it. All I have to do is to take off the wheels and reverse the pawl."

"I—I didn't know mah lawn-moah was named Paul," said the colored man. "Is it writ on it anywhere?"

"No, it's not the kind of Paul you mean," said Tom with a laugh. "It's spelled differently. A pawl is a sort of catch that fits into a ratchet wheel and pushes it around, or it may be used as a catch to prevent the backward motion of a windlass or the wheel on a derrick. I'll have it fixed in a jiffy for you."

Tom worked rapidly. With a monkey-wrench he removed the two big wheels of the lawn-mower and reversed the pawl in the cogs. In five minutes he had replaced the wheels, and the machine, except for needed sharpening, did good work.

"There you are, Rad!" exclaimed Tom at length.

"Yo' suah am a wonder at inventin'!" cried the colored man gratefully. "I'll cut yo' grass all summah fo' yo' to pay fo' this, Mistah Swift."

"Oh, that's too much. I didn't do a great deal, Rad."

"Well, yo' saved me from bein' swindled, Mistah Swift, an' I suah does 'preciate dat."

"How about the fellow you traded the cracked grindstone to, Rad?"

"Oh, well, ef he done run it slow it won't fly apart, an' he'll do dat, anyhow, fo' he suah am a lazy coon. I guess we am about even there, Mistah Swift."

"All right," spoke Tom with a laugh. "Sharpen it up, Rad, and start in to cut grass. It will soon be summer," and Tom, leaping upon his motor-cycle, was off like a shot.

He found his father in his library, reading a book on scientific matters. Mr. Swift looked up in surprise at seeing his son.

"What! Back so soon?" he asked. "You did make a flying trip. Did you give the model and papers to Mr. Crawford?"

"No, dad, I was robbed yesterday. Those scoundrels got ahead of us, after all. They have your model. I tried to telephone to you, but the wires were down, or something."

"What!" cried Mr. Swift. "Oh, Tom! That's too bad! I will lose ten thousand dollars if I can't get that model and those papers back!" and with a despairing gesture Mr. Swift rose and began to pace the floor.

CHAPTER XVIII

HAPPY HARRY AGAIN

Tom watched his father anxiously. The young inventor knew the loss had been a heavy one, and he blamed himself for not having been more careful.

"Tell me all about it, Tom," said Mr. Swift at length. "Are you sure the model and papers are gone? How did it happen?"

Then Tom related what had befallen him.

"Oh, that's too bad!" cried Mr. Swift. "Are you much hurt, Tom? Shall I send for the doctor?" For the time being his anxiety over his son was greater than that concerning his loss.

"No, indeed, dad. I'm all right now. I got a bad blow on the head, but Mrs. Blackford fixed me up. I'm awfully sorry——"

"There, there! Now don't say another word," interrupted Mr. Swift. "It wasn't your fault. It might have happened to me. I dare say it would, for those scoundrels seemed very determined. They are desperate, and will stop at nothing to make good the loss they sustained on the patent motor they exploited. Now they will probably try to make use of my model and papers."

"Do you think they'll do that, dad?"

"Yes. They will either make a motor exactly like mine, or construct one so nearly similar that it will answer their purpose. I will have no redress against them, as my patent is not fully granted yet. Mr. Crawford was to attend to that."

"Can't you do anything to stop them, dad? File an injunction, or something like that?"

"I don't know. I must see Mr. Crawford at once. I wonder if he could come here? He might be able to advise me. I have had very little experience with legal difficulties. My specialty is in other lines of work. But I must do something. Every moment is valuable. I wonder who the men were?"

"I'm sure one of them was the same man who came here that night—the man with the black mustache, who dropped the telegram," said Tom. "I had a pretty good look at him as the auto passed me, and I'm sure it was he. Of course I didn't see who it was that struck me down, but I imagine it was some one of the same gang."

"Very likely. Well, Tom, I must do something. I suppose I might telegraph to Mr. Craw-

ford—he will be expecting you in Albany——
Mr. Swift paused musingly. "No, I have it!" he
suddenly exclaimed. "I'll go to Albany myself."

"Go to Albany, dad?"

"Yes; I must explain everything to the lawyer,
and then he can advise me what to do. Fortunately I have some papers, duplicates of those you
took, which I can show him. Of course the origi-
nals will be necessary before I can prove my claim.
The loss of the model is the most severe, however. Without that I can do little. But I will
have Mr. Crawford take whatever steps are possible. I'll take the night train, Tom. I'll have to
leave you to look after matters here, and I needn't
caution you to be on your guard, though, having
got what they were after, I fancy those financiers,
or their tools, will not bother us again."

"Very likely not," agreed Tom, "but I will keep
my eyes open, just the same. Oh, but that reminds
me, dad. Did you see anything of a tramp around
here while I was away?"

"A tramp? No; but you had better ask Mrs.
Baggert. She usually attends to them. She's so
kind-hearted that she frequently gives them a good
meal."

The housekeeper, when consulted, said that no
tramps had applied in the last few days.

"Why do you ask, Tom?" inquired his father.

"Because I had an experience with one, and I believe he was a member of the same gang whe robbed me." And thereupon Tom told of his encounter with Happy Harry, and how the latter had broken the wire on the motor-cycle.

"You had a narrow escape," commented Mr Swift. "If I had known the dangers involved I would never have allowed you to take the model to Albany."

"Well, I didn't take it there, after all," said Tom with a grim smile, for he could appreciate a joke.

"I must hurry and pack my valise," went on Mr. Swift. "Mrs. Baggert, we will have an early supper, and I will start at once for Albany."

"I wish I could go with you, dad, to make up for the trouble I caused," spoke Tom.

"Tut, tut! Don't talk that way," advised his father kindly. "I will be glad of the trip. It will ease my mind to be doing something."

Tom felt rather lonesome after his father had left, but he laid out a plan of action for himself that he thought would keep him occupied until his father returned. In the first place he made a tour of the house and various machine shops to see that doors and windows were securely fastened.

"What's the matter? Do you expect burglars,

Master Tom?" asked Garret Jackson, the aged engineer.

"Well, Garret, you never can tell," replied the young inventor, as he told of his experience and the necessity for Mr. Swift going to Albany. "Some of those scoundrels, finding how easy it was to rob me, may try it again, and get some of dad's other valuable models. I'm taking no chances."

"That's right, Master Tom. I'll keep steam up in the boiler to-night, though we don't really need it, as your father told me you would probably not run any machinery when he was gone. But with a good head of steam up, and a hose handy, I can give any burglars a hot reception. I almost wish they'd come, so I could get square with them."

"I don't, Garret. Well, I guess everything is in good shape. If you hear anything unusual, or the alarm goes off during the night, call me."

"I will, Master Tom," and the old engineer, who had a living-room in a shack adjoining the boiler-room, locked the door after Tom left.

The young inventor spent the early evening in attaching a new wire to his motor-cycle to replace the one he had purchased while on his disastrous trip. The temporary one was not just the proper thing, though it answered well enough. Then,

having done some work on a new boat propeller
he was contemplating patenting, Tom felt that it
was time to go to bed, as he was tired. He made
a second round of the house, looking to doors and
windows, until Mrs. Baggert exclaimed:

"Oh, Tom, do stop! You make me nervous,
going around that way. I'm sure I shan't sleep a
wink to-night, thinking of burglars and tramps."

Tom laughingly desisted, and went up to his
room. He sat up a few minutes, writing a letter
to a girl of his acquaintance, for, in spite of the
fact that the young inventor was very busy with
his own and his father's work, he found time for
lighter pleasures. Then, as his eyes seemed determined to close of their own accord, if he did
not let them, he tumbled into bed.

Tom fancied it was nearly morning when he
suddenly awoke with a start. He heard a noise,
and at first he could not locate it. Then his trained
ear traced it to the dining-room.

"Why, Mrs. Baggert must be getting breakfast, and is rattling the dishes," he thought. "But
why is she up so early?"

It was quite dark in Tom's room, save for a
little gleam from the crescent moon, and by the
light of this Tom arose and looked at his watch.

"Two o'clock," he whispered. "That can't be

Mrs. Baggert, unless she's sick, and got up to take some medicine."

He listened intently. Below, in the dining-room, he could hear stealthy movements.

"Mrs. Baggert would never move around like that," he decided. "She's too heavy. I wonder— it's a burglar—one of the gang has gotten in!" he exclaimed in tense tones. "I'm going to catch him at it!"

Hurriedly he slipped on some clothes, and then, having softly turned on the electric light in his room, he took from a corner a small rifle, which he made sure was loaded. Then, having taken a small electric flashlight, of the kind used by police-men, and sometimes by burglars, he started on tiptoe toward the lower floor.

As Tom softly descended the stairs he could more plainly hear the movements of the intruder. He made out now that the burglar was in Mr. Swift's study, which opened from the dining-room.

"He's after dad's papers!" thought Tom. "I wonder which one this is?"

The youth had often gone hunting in the woods, and he knew how to approach cautiously. Thus he was able to reach the door of the dining-room without being detected. He had no need to flash his light, for the intruder was doing that so frequently with one he carried that Tom could see him perfectly. The fellow was working at the safe in which Mr. Swift kept his more valuable papers.

Softly, very softly Tom brought his rifle to bear on the back of the thief. Then, holding the weapon with one hand, for it was very light, Tom extended the electric flash, so that the glare would be thrown on the intruder and would leave his own person in the black shadows. Pressing the spring which caused the lantern to throw out a powerful glow, Tom focused the rays on the kneeling man.

"That will be about all!" the youth exclaimed in as steady a voice as he could manage.

The burglar turned like a flash, and Tom had a glimpse of his face. It was the tramp—Happy Harry—whom he had encountered on the lonely road.

CHAPTER XIX

TOM ON A HUNT

Tom held his rifle in readiness, though he only intended it as a means of intimidation, and would not have fired at the burglar except to save his own life. But the sight of the weapon was enough for the tramp. He crouched motionless. His own light had gone out, but by the gleam of the electric he carried Tom could see that the man had in his hand some tool with which he had been endeavoring to force the safe.

"I guess you've got me!" exclaimed the intruder, and there was in his tones no trace of the tramp dialect.

"It looks like it," agreed Tom grimly. "Are you a tramp now, or in some other disguise?"

"Can't you see?" asked the fellow sullenly, and then Tom did notice that the man still had on his tramp make-up.

"What do you want?" asked Tom.

"Hard to tell," replied the burglar calmly. "I

hadn't got the safe open before you came down and disturbed me. I'm after money, naturally."

"No, you're not!" exclaimed Tom.

"What's that?" and the man seemed surprised.

"No, you're not!" went on Tom, and he held his rifle in readiness. "You're after the patent papers and the model of the turbine motor. But it's gone. Your confederates got it away from me. They probably haven't told you yet, and you're still on the hunt for it. You'll not get it, but I've got you."

"So I see," admitted Happy Harry, and he spoke with some culture. "If you don't mind," he went on, "would you just as soon move that gun a little? It's pointing right at my head, and it might go off."

"It is going off—very soon!" exclaimed Tom grimly, and the tramp started in alarm. "Oh, I'm not going to shoot you," continued the young inventor. "I'm going to fire this as an alarm, and the engineer will come in here and tie you up. Then I'm going to hand you over to the police. This rifle is a repeater, and I am a pretty good shot. I'm going to fire once now, to summon assistance, and if you try to get away I'll be ready to fire a second time, and that won't be so comfortable for you. I've caught you, and I'm going to hold on to you until I get that model and those papers back."

"Oh, you are, eh?" asked the burglar calmly. "Well, all I've got to say is that you have grit. Go ahead. I'm caught good and proper. I was foolish to come in here, but I thought I'd take a chance."

"Who are you, anyhow? Who are the men working with you to defraud my father of his rights?" asked Tom somewhat bitterly.

"I'll never tell you," answered the burglar. "I was hired to do certain work, and that's all there is to it. I'm not going to peach on my pals."

"We'll see about that!" burst out Tom. Then he noticed that a dining-room window behind where the burglar was kneeling was open. Doubtless the intruder had entered that way, and intended to escape in the same manner.

"I'm going to shoot," announced Tom, and, aiming his rifle at the open window, where the bullet would do no damage, he pressed the trigger. He noticed that the burglar was crouching low down on the floor, but Tom thought nothing of this at the time. He imagined that Happy Harry—or whatever his name was—might be afraid of getting hit.

There was a flash of fire and a deafening report as Tom fired. The cloud of smoke obscured his

vision for a moment, and as the echoes died away
Tom could hear Mrs. Baggert screaming in her
room.

"It's all right!" cried the young inventor re-
assuringly. "No one is hurt, Mrs. Baggert!"
Then he flashed his light on the spot where the
burglar had crouched. As the smoke rolled away
Tom peered in vain for a sight of the intruder.

Happy Harry was gone!

Holding his rifle in readiness, in case he should
be attacked from some unexpected quarter, Tom
strode forward. He flashed his light in every
direction. There was no doubt about it. The
intruder had fled. Taking advantage of the noise
when the gun was fired, and under cover of the
smoke, the burglar had leaped from the open window. Tom guessed as much. He hurried to the
casement and peered out, at the same time noticing
the cut wire of the burglar alarm. It was quite
dark, and he fancied he could hear the noise of
some one running rapidly. Aiming his rifle into
the air, he fired again, at the same time crying
out:

"Hold on!"

"All right, Master Tom, I'm coming!" called
the voice of the engineer from his shack. "Are
you hurt? Is Mrs. Baggert murdered? I hear
her screaming."

"That's pretty good evidence that she isn't murdered," said Tom with a grim smile.

"Are you hurt?" again called Mr. Jackson.

"No, I'm all right," answered Tom. "Did you see any one running away as you came up?"

"No, Master Tom, I didn't. What happened?"

"A burglar got in, and I had him cornered, but he got away when I fired to arouse you."

By this time the engineer was at the stoop, on which the window opened. Tom unlocked a side door and admitted Mr. Jackson, and then, the incandescent light having been turned on, the two looked around the apartment. Nothing in it had been disturbed, and the safe had not been opened.

"I heard him just in time," commented Tom, telling the engineer what had happened. "I wish I had thought to get between him and the window. Then he couldn't have gotten away."

"He might have injured you, though," said Mr. Jackson. "We'll go outside now, and look——"

"Is any one killed? Are you both murdered?" cried Mrs. Baggert at the dining-room door. "If any one is killed I'm not coming in there. I can't bear the sight of blood."

"No one is hurt," declared Tom with a laugh. "Come on in, Mrs. Baggert," and the housekeeper entered, her hair all done up in curl papers.

"Oh, my goodness me!" she exclaimed. "When I heard that cannon go off I was sure the house was coming down. How is it some one wasn't killed?"

"That wasn't a cannon; it was only my little rifle," said Tom, and then he told again, for the benefit of the housekeeper, the story of what had happened.

"We'd better hurry and look around the premises," suggested Mr. Jackson. "Maybe he is hiding, and will come back, or perhaps he has some confederates on the watch."

"Not much danger of that," declared Tom. "Happy Harry is far enough away from here now, and so are his confederates, if he had any, which I doubt. Still, it will do no harm to take a look around."

A search resulted in nothing, however, and the Swift household had soon settled down again, though no one slept soundly during the remainder of the night.

In the morning Tom sent word of what had happened to the police of Shopton. Some officers came out to the house, but, beyond looking wisely at the window by which the burglar had entered and at some footprints in the garden, they could do nothing. Tom wanted to go off on his motor-cycle on a tour of the surrounding neighborhood to see if he could get any clues, but he did not think it would be wise in the absence of his father. He thought it would be better to remain at home, in case any further efforts were made to get possession of valuable models or papers.

"There's not much likelihood of that, though," said Tom to the old engineer. "Those fellows have what they want, and are not going to bother us again. I would like to get that model back for dad, though. If they file it and take out a patent, even if he can prove that it is his, it will mean a long lawsuit and he may be defrauded of his rights, after all. Possession is nine points of the law, and part of the tenth, too, I guess."

So Tom remained at home and busied himself as well as he could over some new machines he was constructing. He got a telegram from his father that afternoon, stating that Mr. Swift had safely arrived in Albany, and would return the following day.

"Did you have any luck, dad?" asked the young inventor, when his father, tired and worn from the unaccustomed traveling, reached home in the evening.

"Not much, Tom," was the reply. "Mr. Crawford has gone back to Washington, and he is going to do what he can to prevent those men taking advantage of me."

"Did you get any trace of the thieves? Does Mr. Crawford think he can?"

"No to both questions. His idea is that the men will remain in hiding for a while, and then, when the matter has quieted down, they will proceed to get a patent on the motor that I invented."

"But, in the meanwhile, can't you make another model and get a patent yourself?"

"No; there are certain legal difficulties in the way. Besides, those men have the original papers I need. As for the model, it will take me nearly a year to build a new one that will work properly, as it is very complicated. I am afraid, Tom, that all my labor on the turbine motor is thrown away. Those scoundrels will reap the benefit of it."

"Oh, I hope not, dad! I'm sure those fellows will be caught. Now that you are back home again, I'm going out on a hunt on my own account. I don't put much faith in the police. It was through me, dad, that you lost your model and the papers, and I'll get them back!"

"No, you must not think it was your fault, Tom," said his father. "You could not help it, though I appreciate your desire to recover the missing model."

"And I'll do it, too, dad. I'll start to-morrow, and I'll make a complete circuit of the country for a hundred miles around. I can easily do it on my motor-cycle. If I can't get on the trail of the three men who robbed me, maybe I can find Happy Harry."

"I doubt it, my son. Still, you may try. Now I must write to Mr. Crawford and tell him about the attempted burglary while I was away. It may give him a clue to work on. I'm afraid you ran quite a risk, Tom."

"I didn't think about that, dad. I only wish I had managed to keep that rascal a prisoner."

The next day Tom started off on a hunt. He planned to be gone overnight, as he intended to go first to Dunkirk, where Mr. Blackford lived, and begin his search from there.

CHAPTER XX

ERADICATE SAWS WOOD

THE farmer's family, including the son who was a deputy sheriff, was glad to see Tom. Jed said he had "been on the job" ever since the mysterious robbery of Tom had taken place, but though he had seen many red automobiles he had no trace of the three men.

From Dunkirk Tom went back over the route he had taken in going from Pompville to Centreford, and made some inquiries in the neighborhood of the church shed, where he had taken shelter. The locality was sparsely settled, however, and no one could give any clues to the robbers.

The young inventor next made a trip over the lonely, sandy road, where he had met with the tramp, Happy Harry. But there were even fewer houses near that stretch than around the church, so he got no satisfaction there. Tom spent the night at a country inn, and resumed his search the next morning, but with no results. The men

159

had apparently completely disappeared, leaving no traces behind them.

"I may as well go home," thought Tom, as he was riding his motor-cycle along a pleasant country road. "Dad may be worried, and perhaps something has turned up in Shopton that will aid me. If there isn't, I'm going to start out again in a few days in another direction."

There was no news in Shopton, however. Tom found his father scarcely able to work, so worried was he over the loss of his most important invention.

Two weeks passed, the young machinist taking trips of several days' duration to different points near his home, in the hope of discovering something. But he was unsuccessful, and, in the meanwhile, no reassuring word was received from the lawyers in Washington. Mr. Crawford wrote that no move had yet been made by the thieves to take out patent papers, and while this, in a sense, was some aid to Mr. Swift, still he could not proceed on his own account to protect his new motor. All that could be done was to await the first movement on the part of the scoundrels.

"I think I'll try a new plan to-morrow, dad," announced Tom one night, when he and his father had talked over again, for perhaps the twentieth time, the happenings of the last few weeks.

"What is it, Tom?" asked the inventor.

"Well, I think I'll take a week's trip on my machine. I'll visit all the small towns around here, but, instead of asking in houses for news of the tramp or his confederates, I'll go to the police and constables. I'll ask if they have arrested any tramps recently, and, if they have, I'll ask them to let me see the 'hobo' prisoners."

"What good will that do?"

"I'll tell you. I have an idea that though the burglar who got in here may not be a regular tramp, yet he disguises himself like one at times, and may be known to other tramps. If I can get on the trail of Happy Harry, as he calls himself, I may locate the other men. Tramps would be very likely to remember such a peculiar chap as Happy Harry, and they will tell me where they had last seen him. Then I will have a starting point."

"Well, that may be a good plan," assented Mr. Swift. "At any rate it will do no harm to try. A tramp locked up in a country police station will very likely be willing to talk. Go ahead with that scheme, Tom, but don't get into any danger. How long will you be away?"

"I don't know. A week, perhaps; maybe longer. I'll take plenty of money with me, and stop at country hotels overnight."

Tom lost no time in putting his plan into execution. He packed some clothes in a grip, which he attached to the rear of his motor-cycle, and then having said good-by to his father, started off. The first three days he met with no success. He located several tramps in country lock-ups, where they had been sent for begging or loitering, but none of them knew Happy Harry or had ever heard of a tramp answering his description.

"He ain't one of us, youse can make up your mind to dat," said one "hobo" whom Tom interviewed. "No real knight of de highway goes around in a disguise. We leaves dat for de story book detectives. I'm de real article, I am, an' I don't know Happy Harry. But, fer dat matter, any of us is happy enough in de summer time, if we don't strike a burgh like dis, where dey jugs you fer panhandlin'."

In general, Tom found the tramp willing enough to answer his questions, though some were sullen, and returned only surly growls to his inquiries.

"I guess I'll have to give it up and go back home," he decided one night. But there was a small town, not many miles from Shopton, which he had not yet visited, and he resolved to try there before returning. Accordingly, the next morning found him inquiring of the police authorities in

Meadton. But no tramps had been arrested in the last month, and no one had seen anything of a tramp like Happy Harry or three mysterious men in an automobile.

Tom was beginning to despair. Riding along a silent road, that passed through a strip of woods, he was trying to think of some new line of procedure, when the silence of the highway, that, hitherto, had resounded only with the muffled explosions of his machine, was broken by several exclamations.

"Now, Boomerang, yo' might jest as well start now as later," Tom heard a voice saying—a voice he recognized well. "Yo' hab got t' do dis yean wuk, an' dere ain't no gittin' out ob it. Dis yeah wood am got to be sawed, an' yo' hab got to saw it. But it am jest laik yo' to go back on yo' ole friend Eradicate in dis yeah fashion. I neber could tell what yo' were gwine t' do next, an' I cain't now. G'lang, now, won't yo'? Let's git dis yeah sawmill started."

Tom shut off the power and leaped from his wheel. From the woods at his left came the protesting "hee-haw" of a mule.

"Boomerang and Eradicate Sampson!" exclaimed the young inventor. "What can they be doing here?"

He leaned his motor-cycle against the fence and

advanced toward where he had heard the voice of the colored man. In a little clearing he saw him. Eradicate was presiding over a portable sawmill, worked by a treadmill, on the incline of which was the mule, its ears laid back, and an unmistakable expression of anger on its face.

"Why, Rad, what are you doing?" cried Tom.

"Good land o' massy! Ef it ain't young Mistah Swift!" cried the darky. "Howdy, Mistah Swift! Howdy! I'm jest tryin' t' saw some wood, t' make a .ivin', but Boomerang he doan't seem t' want t' lib," and with that Eradicate looked reproachfully at the animal.

"What seems to be the trouble, and how did you come to own this sawmill?" asked Tom.

"I'll tell you', Mistah Swift, I'll tell you,' spoke Eradicate. "Sit right yeah on dis log, an' I'll explanation it to yo'."

"The last time I saw you, you were preparing to go into the grass-cutting business," went on Tom.

"Yais, sah! Dat's right. So I was. Yo' has got a memory, yo' suah has. But it am dis yeah way. Grass ain't growin' quick enough, an' so I traded off dat lawn-moah an' bought dis yeah mill. But now it won't go, an' I suah am in trouble," and once more Eradicate Sampson looked indignantly at Boomerang.

CHAPTER XXI

ERADICATE GIVES A CLUE

"TELL me all about it," urged Tom sympathetically, for he had a friendly feeling toward the aged darky.

"Well," began Eradicate, "I suah thought I were gwine to make money cuttin' grass, 'specially after yo' done fixed mah moah. But 'peared laik nobody wanted any grass cut. I trabeled all ober, an' I couldn't git no jobs. Now me an' Boomerang has to eat, no mattah ef he is contrary, so I had t' look fo' some new wuk. I traded dat lawn-moah off fo' a cross-cut saw, but dat was such hard wuk dat I gib it up. Den I got a chance to buy dis yeah outfit cheap, an' I bought it."

Eradicate then went on to tell how he had purchased the portable sawmill from a man who had no further use for it, and how he had managed to transport it from a distant village to the spot where Tom had met him. There he had secured permission to work a piece of woodland on shares, sawing up the smaller trees into cord wood. He had started in well enough, cutting down considerable timber, for the colored man was a willing worker, but when he tried to start his mill he met with trouble.

"I counted on Boomerang helpin' me," he said to Tom. "All he has to do is walk on dat tread-mill, an' keep goin'. Dat makes de saw go 'round, an' I saws de wood. But de trouble am dat I can't git Boomerang to move. I done tried ebery means I knows on, an' he won't go. I talked kind to him, an' I talked harsh. I done beat him wif a club, an' I rub his ears soft laik, an' he allers did laik dat, but he won't go. I fed him on carrots an' I gib him sugar, an' I eben starve him, but he won't go. Heah I been tryin' fo' three days now t' git him started, an' not a stick hab I sawed. De man what I'm wukin' wif on shares he git mad, an' he say ef I doan't saw wood pretty soon he gwine t' git annuder mill heah. Now I axes yo' fair, Mistah Swift, ain't I got lots ob trouble?"

"You certainly seem to have," agreed Tom "But why is Boomerang so obstinate? Usually on a treadmill a horse or a mule has to work whether they like it or not. If they don't keep moving the platform slides out from under them, and they come up against the back bar."

"Dat's what done happened to Boomerang," declared Eradicate. "He done back up against de bar, an' dere he stay."

Tom went over and looked at the mill. The outfit was an old one, and had seen much service, but the trained eye of the young inventor saw that it could still be used effectively. Boomerang watched Tom, as though aware that something unusual was about to happen.

"Heah I done gone an' 'vested mah money in dis yeah mill," complained Eradicate, "an' I ain't sawed up a single stick. Ef I wasn't so kind-hearted I'd chastise dat mule wuss dan I has, dat's what I would."

Tom said nothing. He was stooping down, looking at the gearing that connected the tread-mill with the shaft which revolved the saw. Suddenly he uttered an exclamation.

"Rad, have you been monkeying with this machinery?" he asked.

Me? Good land, Mistah Swift, no, sah! I wouldn't tech it. It's jest as I got it from de man I bought it ob. It worked when he had it, but he used a hoss. It's all due to de contrariness ob Boomerang, an' if I——"

"No, it isn't the mule's fault at all!" exclaimed Tom. "The mill is out of gear, and tread is locked; that's all. The man you bought it of

probably did it so you could haul it along the
road. I'll have it fixed for you in a few minutes.
Wait until I get some tools."

From the bag on his motor-cycle Tom got his
implements. He first unlocked the treadmill, so
that the inclined platform, on which the animal
slowly walked, could revolve. No sooner had he
done this than Boomerang, feeling the slats under
his hoofs moving away, started forward. With a
rattle the treadmill slid around.

"Good land o' massy! It's goin'!" cried Eradicate delightedly. "It suah am goin'!" he added
as he saw the mule, with nimble feet, send the
revolving, endless string of slats around and
around. "But de saw doan't move, Mistah Swift.
Yo' am pretty sma t at fixin' it as much as yo'
has, but 1 reckor it's too busted t' eber saw any
wood. I'se got bad luck, dat's what I has."

"Nonsense!" exclaimed Tom. "The sawmill
will be going in a moment. All I have to do is
to throw it into gear. See here, Rad. When
you want the saw to go you just throw this handle forward. That makes the gears mesh."

"What's dat 'bout mush?" asked Eradicate.

"Mesh—not mush. I mean it makes the cogs
fit together. See," and Tom pressed the lever.
In an instant, with a musical whirr, the saw began
revolving.

"Hurrah! Dere it goes! Golly! see dat saw move!" cried the delighted colored man. He seized a stick of wood, and in a trice it was sawed through.

"Whoop!" yelled Eradicate. "I'm sabed now! Bless yo', Mistah Swift, yo' suttinly am a wondah!"

"Now I'll show you how it works," went on Tom. "When you want to stop Boomerang, you just pull this handle. That locks the tread, and he can't move it," and, suiting the action to his words, Tom stopped the mill. "Then," he went on, "when you want him to move, you pull the handle this way," and he showed the darky how to do it. In a moment the mule was moving again. Then Tom illustrated how to throw the saw in and out of gear, and in a few minutes the sawmill was in full operation, with a most energetic colored man feeding in logs to be cut up into stove lengths.

"You ought to have an assistant, Rad," said Tom, after he had watched the work for a while. "You could get more done then, and move on to some other wood-patch."

"Dat's right, Mistah Swift, so I had. But I done tried, an' couldn't git any. I ast seberal colored men, but dey'd radder whitewash an' clean chicken coops. I guess I'll hab t' go it alone. I ast a white man yisterday ef he wouldn't like t' pitch in an' help, but he said he didn't like to wuk. He was a tramp, an' he had de nerve to ask me fer money—me, a hard-wukin' coon."

"You didn't give it to him, I hope."

"No, indeedy, but he come so close to me dat I was askeered he might take it from me, so I kept hold ob a club. He suah was a bad-lookin' tramp, an' he kept laffin'" all de while, like he was happy."

"What's that?" cried Tom, struck by the words of the colored man. "Did he have a thick, brown beard?"

"Dat's what he had," answered Eradicate, pausing in the midst of his work. "He suah were a funny sort ob tramp. His hands done looked laik he neber wuked, an' he had a funny blue ring one finger, only it wasn't a reg'lar ring, yo' know. It was pushed right inter his skin, laik a man I seen at de circus once, all cobered wid funny figgers."

Tom leaped to his feet.

"Which finger was the blue ring tattooed on?" he asked, and he waited anxiously for the answer.

"Let me see, it were on de right—no, it were on de little finger ob de left hand."

"Are you sure, Rad?"

"Suah, Mistah Swift. I took 'tic'lar notice, 'cause he carried a stick in dat same hand."

"It must be my man—Happy Harry!" exclaimed Tom half aloud. "Which way did he go, Rad, after he left you?"

"He went up de lake shore," replied the colored man. "He asked me if I knowed ob an ole big house up dere, what nobody libed in, an' I said I did. Den he left, an' I were glad ob it."

"Which house did you mean, Rad?"

"Why, dat ole mansion what General Harkness used t' lib in befo' de wah. Dere ain't nobody libed in it fo' some years now, an' it's deserted. Maybe a lot ob tramps stays in it, an' dat's where dis man were goin'."

"Maybe," assented Tom, who was all excitement now. "Just where is this old house, Rad?"

"Away up at de head ob Lake Carlopa. I uster wuk dere befo' de wah, but it's been a good many years since quality folks libed dere. Why, did yo' want t' see dat man, Mistah Swift?"

"Yes, Rad, I did, and very badly, too. I think he is the very person I want. But don't say anything about it. I'm going to take a trip up to that strange mansion. Maybe I'll get on the trail of Happy Harry and the men who robbed me. I'm much obliged to you, Rad, for this information. It's a good clue, I think. Strange that you should meet the very tramp I've been searching for."

"Well, I suah am obliged to yo', Mistah Swift, fo' fixin' mah sawmill."

"That's all right. What you told me more than pays for what I did, Rad. Well, I'm going home now to tell dad, and then I'm going to start out. Yesterday, you said it was, you saw Happy Harry? Well, I'll get right after him," and leaving a somewhat surprised, but very much delighted, colored man behind him, Tom mounted his motor-cycle and started for home at a fast pace.

CHAPTER XXII

THE STRANGE MANSION

"DAD, I've got a clue!" exclaimed Tom, hurrying into the house late that afternoon, following a quick trip from where he had met Eradicate with his sawmill. "A good clue, and I'm going to start early in the morning to run it down."

"Wait a minute, now, Tom," cautioned his father slowly. "You know what happens when you get excited. Nothing good was ever done in a hurry."

"Well, I can't help being excited, dad. I think I'm on the trail of those scoundrels. I almost wish I could start to-night."

"Suppose you tell me all about it," and Mr. Swift laid aside a scientific book he was reading.

Whereupon Tom told of his meeting with the colored man, and what Eradicate had said about the tramp.

"But he may not be the same Happy Harry you are looking for," interposed Mr. Swift.

"Tramps who don't like to work, and who have a jolly disposition, also those who ask for money and have designs tattooed on their hands, are very common."

"Oh, but I'm sure this is the same one," declared Tom. "He wants to stay in this neighborhood until he locates his confederates. That's why he's hanging around. Now I have an idea that the deserted mansion, where Eradicate used to work, and which once housed Gener..i Harkness and his family, is the rendezvous of this gang of thieves."

"You are taking a great deal for granted, Tom."

"I don't think so, dad. I've got to assume something, and maybe I'm wrong, but I don't think so. At any rate, I'm going to try, if you'll let me."

"What do you mean to do?"

"I want to go to that deserted mansion and see what I can find. If I locate the thieves, well——"

"You may run into danger."

"Then you admit I may be on the right track, dad?"

"Not at all," and Mr. Swift smiled at the quick manner in which Tom turned the tables on him. "I admit there may be a band of tramps in that house. Very likely there is—almost any deserted place would be attractive to them. But they may not be the ones you seek. In fact, I hardly see how they can be. The men who stole my model and patent papers are wealthy. They would not be very likely to stay in deserted houses."

"Perhaps some of the scoundrels whom they hired might, and through them I can get on the track of the principals."

"Well, there is something in that," admitted Mr. Swift.

"Then may I go, dad?"

"I suppose so. We must leave nothing untried to get back the stolen model and papers. But I don't want you to run any risks. If you would only take some one with you. There's your chum, Ned Newton. Perhaps he would go."

"No, I'd rather work it alone, dad. I'll be careful. Besides, Ned could not get away from the bank. I may have to be gone a week, and he has no motor-cycle. I can manage all right."

Tom was off bright and early. He had carefully laid his plans, and had decided that he would not go direct to Pineford, which was the nearest village to the old Harkness mansion.

"If those fellows are in hiding they will probably keep watch on who comes to the village," thought Tom. "The arrival of some one on a motor-cycle will be sure to be reported to them, and they may skip out. I've got to come up from another direction, so I think I'll circle around, and reach the mansion from the stretch of woods on the north."

He had inquired from Eradicate as to the lay of the land, and had a good general idea of it. He knew there was a patch of woodland on one side of the mansion, while the other sides were open.

"I may not be able to ride through the woods," mused Tom, "but I'll take my machine as close as I can, and walk the rest of the way. Once I discover whether or not the gang is in the place, I'll know what to do."

To follow out the plan he had laid down for himself meant that Tom must take a roundabout way. It would necessitate being a whole day on the road, before he would be near the head of Lake Carlopa, where the Harkness house was located. The lake was a large one, and Tom had never been to the upper end.

When he was within a few miles of Pineford, Tom took a road that branched off and went around it. Stopping at night in a lonely farm-house, he pushed on the next morning, hoping to get to the woods that night. But a puncture to one of the tires delayed him, and after that was repaired he discovered something wrong with his batteries. He had to go five miles out of his way to get new cells, and it was dusk when he came to the stretch of woods which he knew lay between him and the old mansion.

"I don't fancy starting in there at night," said Tom to himself. "Guess I'd better stay somewhere around here until morning, and then venture in. But the question is where to stay?"

The country was deserted, and for a mile or more he had seen no houses. He kept on for some distance farther, the dusk falling rapidly, and when he was about to turn back to retrace his way to the last farmhouse he had passed, he saw a slab shanty at the side of the road.

"That's better than nothing, provided they'll take me in for the night," murmured Tom. "I'm going to ask, anyhow."

He found the shanty to be inhabited by an old man who made a living burning charcoal. The place was not very attractive, but Tom did not mind that, and finding the charcoal-burner a kindly old fellow, soon made a bargain with him to remain all night.

Tom slept soundly, in spite of his strange surroundings, and after a simple breakfast in the morning inquired of the old man the best way of penetrating the forest.

"You'd best strike right along the old wood road," said the charcoal-burner. "That leads right to the lake, and I think will take you where you want to go. The old mansion is not far from the lake shore."

"Near the lake, eh?" mused Tom as he started off, after thanking the old fellow. "Now I wonder if I'd better try to get to it from the water or the land side?"

He found it impossible to ride fast on the old wood road, and when he judged he was so close to the lake that the noise of his motor-cycle might be heard, he shut off the power, and walked along, pushing it. It was hard traveling, and he felt weary, but he kept on, and about noon was rewarded by a sight of something glittering through the trees.

"That's the lake!" Tom exclaimed, half aloud. "I'm almost there."

A little later, having hidden his motor-cycle in a clump of bushes, he made his way through the underbrush and stood on the shore of Lake Carlopa. Cautiously Tom looked about him. It was getting well on in the afternoon, and the sun was striking across the broad sheet of water. Tom glanced up along the shore. Something amid a clump of trees caught his eyes. It was the chimney of a house. The young inventor walked a little distance along the lake shore. Suddenly he saw, looming up in the forest, a large building. It needed but a glance to show that it was falling into ruins, and had no signs of life about it. Nor, for that matter, was there any life in the forest around him, or on the lake that stretched out before him.

"I wonder if that can be the place?" whispered Tom, for, somehow, the silence of the place was getting on his nerves. "It must be it," he went on. "It's just as Rad described it."

He stood looking at it, the sun striking full on the mysterious mansion, hidden there amid the trees. Suddenly, as Tom looked, he heard the "put-put" of a motor-boat. He turned to one side, and saw, putting out from a little dock that he had not noticed before, a small craft. It contained one man, and no sooner had the young inventor caught a glimpse of him than he cried out:

"That's the man who jumped over our fence and escaped!"

Then, before the occupant of the boat could catch sight of him, Tom turned and fled back into the bushes, out of view.

CHAPTER XXIII

TOM IS PURSUED

Tom was so excited that he hardly knew what to do. His first thought was to keep out of sight of the man in the boat, for the young inventor did not want the criminals to suspect that he was on their trail. To that end he ran back until he knew he could not be seen from the lake. There he paused and peered through the bushes. He caught a glimpse of the man in the motor-boat. The craft was making fast time across the water.

"He didn't see me," murmured Tom. "Lucky I saw him first. Now what had I better do?"

It was a hard question to answer. If he only had some one with whom to consult he would have felt better, but he knew he had to rely on himself. Tom was a resourceful lad, and he had often before been obliged to depend on his wits. But this time very much was at stake, and a false move might ruin everything.

"This is certainly the house," went on Tom,

"and that man in the boat is one of the fellows who helped rob me. Now the next thing to do is to find out if the others of the gang are in the old mansion, and, if they are, to see if dad's model and papers are there. Then the next thing to do will be to get our things away, and I fancy I'll have no easy job."

Well might Tom think this, for the men with whom he had to deal were desperate characters, who had already dared much to accomplish their ends, and who would do more before they would suffer defeat. Still, they under-estimated the pluck of the lad who was pitted against them.

"I might as well proceed on a certain plan, and have some system about this affair," reasoned the lad. "Dad is a great believer in system, so I'll lay out a plan and see how nearly I can follow it. Let's see—what is the first thing to do?"

Tom considered a moment, going over the whole situation in his mind. Then he went on, talking to himself alone there in the woods:

"It seems to me the first thing to do is to find out if the men are in the house. To do that I've got to get closer and look in through a window. Now, how to get closer?"

He considered that problem from all sides.

"It will hardly do to approach from the lake shore," he reasoned. "for if they have a motor-boat and a dock, there must be a path from the house to the water. If there is a path people are likely to walk up or down it at any minute. The man in the boat might come back unexpectedly and catch me. No, I can't risk approaching from the lake shore. I've got to work my way up to the house by going through the woods. That much is settled. Now to approach the house, and when I get within seeing distance I'll settle the next point. One thing at a time is a good rule, as dad used to say. Poor dad! I do hope I can get his model and papers back for him."

Tom, who had been sitting on a log under a bush, staring at the lake, arose. He was feeling rather weak and faint, and was at a loss to account for it, until he remembered that he had had no dinner.

"And I'm not likely to get any," he remarked. "I'm not going to eat until I see who's in that house. Maybe I won't then, and where supper is coming from I don't know. But this is too important to be considered in the same breath with a meal. Here goes."

Cautiously Tom made his way forward, taking care not to make too much disturbance in the bushes. He had been on hunting trips, and knew the value of silence in the woods. He had no paths to follow, but he had noted the position of

the sun, and though that luminary was now sink-
ing lower and lower in the west, he could see the
gleam of it through the trees, and knew in which
direction from it lay the deserted mansion.

Tom moved slowly, and stopped every now and
then to listen. All the sounds he heard were those
made by the creatures of the woods—birds, squir-
rels and rabbits. He went forward for half an
hour, though in that time he did not cover much
ground, and he was just beginning to think that
the house must be near at hand when through a
fringe of bushes he saw the old mansion. It
stood in the midst of what had once been a fine
park, but which was now overgrown with weeds
and tangled briars. The paths that led to the
house were almost out of sight, and the once
beautiful home was partly in ruins.

"I guess I can sneak up there and take a look
in one of the windows," thought the young inventor. He was about to advance, when he suddenly stopped. He heard some one or some thing
coming around the corner of the mansion. A
moment later a man came into view, and Tom
easily recognized him as one of those who
had been in the automobile. The heart of the
young inventor beat so hard that he was afraid
the man would hear it, and Tom crouched down
in the bushes to keep out of sight. The man evi-

dently did not suspect the presence of a stranger, for, though he cast sharp glances into the tangled undergrowth that fringed the house like a hedge, he did not seek to investigate further. He walked slowly on, making a circuit of the grounds. Tom remained hidden for several minutes, and was about to proceed again, when the man reappeared. Then Tom saw the reason for it.

"He's on guard!" the lad said to himself. "He's doing sentry duty. I can't approach the house when he's there."

For an instant Tom felt a bitter disappointment. He had hoped to be able to carry out his plan as he had mapped it. Now he would have to make a change.

"I'll have to wait until night," he thought. "Then I can sneak up and look in. The guard won't see me after dark. But it's going to be no fun to stay here, without anything to eat. Still, I've got to do it."

He remained where he was in the bushes. Several times, before the sun set, the man doing sentry duty made the circuit of the house, and Tom noted that occasionally he was gone for a long period. He reasoned that the man had gone into the mansion to confer with his confederates.

"If I only knew what was going on in there," thought Tom. "Maybe, after all, the men haven't got the model and papers here. Yet, if they haven't, why are they staying in the old house? I must get a look in and see what's going on. Lucky there are no shades to the windows. I wish it would get dark."

It seemed that the sun would never go down and give place to dusk, but finally Tom, crouching in his hiding place, saw the shadows grow longer and longer, and finally the twilight of the woods gave place to a density that was hard to penetrate. Tom waited some time to see if the guard kept up the circuit, but with the approach of night the man seemed to have gone into the house. Tom saw a light gleam out from the lonely mansion. It came from a window on the ground floor.

"There's my chance!" exclaimed the lad, and, crawling from his hiding place, he advanced cautiously toward it.

Tom went forward only a few feet at a time, pausing almost every other step to listen. He heard no sounds, and was reassured. Nearer and nearer he came to the old house. The gleam of the light fell upon his face, and fearful that some one might be looking from the window, he shifted his course, so as to come up from one side. Slowly, very slowly he advanced, until he was right under the window. Then he found that it was too high up to admit of his looking in. He felt about until he had a stone to stand on.

Softly he drew himself up inch by inch. He could hear the murmur of voices in the room. Now the top of his head was on a level with the sill. A few more inches and his eyes could take in the room and the occupants. He was scarcely breathing. Up, up he raised himself until he could look into the apartment, and the sight which met his eyes nearly caused him to lose his hold and topple backward.

For grouped around a table in a big room were the three men whom he had seen in the automobile. But what attracted his attention more than the sight of the men was an object on the table. It was the stolen model! The men were inspecting it, and operating it, as he could see. One of the trio had a bundle of papers in his hand, and Tom was sure they were the ones stolen from him. But there could be no doubt about the model of the turbine motor. There it was in plain sight. He had tracked the thieves to their hiding place.

Then, as he watched, Tom saw one of the men produce from under the table a box, into which the model was placed. The papers were next put in, and a cover was nailed on. Then the men appeared to consult among themselves.

By their gestures Tom concluded that they

were debating where to hide the box. One man pointed toward the lake, and another toward the forest. Tom was edging himself up farther, in order to see better, and, if possible, catch their words, when his foot slipped, and he made a slight noise. Instantly the men turned toward the window, but Tom had stooped down out of sight, just in time.

A moment later, however, he heard some one approaching through the woods behind him, and a voice called out:

"What are you doing? Get away from there!"

Rapid footsteps sounded, and Tom, in a panic, turned and fled, with an unknown pursuer after him.

CHAPTER XXIV

UNEXPECTED HELP

TOM rushed on through the woods. The ..ghted room into which he had been looking had temporarily blinded him when it came to plunging into the darkness again, and he could not see where he was going. He crashed f--"-tilt into a tree, and was thrown backward. Bruised and cut, he picked himself up and rushed off in another direction. Fortunately he struck into some sort of a path, probably one made by cows, and then, as his eyes recovered their faculties, he could dimly distinguish the trees on either side of him and avoid them.

His heart, that was beating fiercely, calmed down after his first fright, and when he had run on for several minutes he stopped.

"That—that must—have been—the—the man —from the boat," panted our hero, whispering to himself. "He came back and saw me. I wonder if he's after me yet?"

Tom listened. The only sound he could hear was the trill and chirp of the insects of the woods. The pursuit, which had lasted only a few minutes, was over. But it might be resumed at any moment. Tom was not safe yet, he thought, and he kept on.

"I wonder where I am? I wonder where my motor-cycle is? I wonder what I had better do?" he asked himself.

Three big questions, and no way of settling them. Tom pulled himself up sharply.

"I've got to think this thing out," he resumed. "They can't find me in these woods to-night, that's sure, unless they get dogs, and they're not likely to do that. So I'm safe that far. But that's about all that is in my favor. I won't dare to go back to the house, even if I could find it in this blackness, which is doubtful. It wouldn't be safe, for they'll be on guard now. It looks as though I was up against it. I'm afraid they may imagine the police are after them, and go away. If they do, and take the model and papers with them, I'll have an awful job to locate them again, and probably I won't be able to. That's the worst of it. Here I have everything right under my hands, and I can't do a thing. If I only had some one to help me; some one to leave on guard while I went for the police. I'm one against three—no, four, for the man in the boat is back. Let's see what can I do?"

Then a sudden plan came to him.

"The lake shore!" he exclaimed, half aloud. "I'll go down there and keep watch. If they escape they'll probably go in the boat, for they wouldn't venture through the woods at night. That's it. I'll watch on shore, and if they do leave in the boat——" He paused again, undecided. "Why, if they do," he finished, "I'll sing out, and make such a row that they'll think the whole countryside is after them. That may drive them back, or they may drop the box containing the papers and model, and cut for it. If they do I'll be all right. I don't care about capturing them, if I can get dad's model back."

He felt more like himself, now that he had mapped out another plan.

"The first thing to do is to locate the lake," reasoned Tom. "Let's see; I ran in a straight line away from the house—that is, as nearly straight as I could. Now if I turn around and go straight back, bearing off a little to the left, I ought to come to the water. I'll do it."

But it was not so easy as Tom imagined, and several times he found himself in the midst of almost impenetrable bushes. He kept on, however, and soon had the satisfaction of emerging from the woods out on the shore of the lake. Then, having gotten his bearings as well as he could in the darkness, he moved down until he was near the deserted house. The light was still showing from the window, and Tom judged by this that the men had not taken fright and fled.

"I suppose I could sneak down and set the motor-boat adrift," he argued. "That would prevent them leaving by way of the lake, anyhow. That's what I'll do! I'll cut off one means of escape. I'll set the boat adrift!"

Very cautiously he advanced toward where he had seen the small craft put out. He was on his guard, for he feared the men would be on the watch, but he reached the dock in safety, and was loosening the rope that tied the boat to the little wharf when another thought came to him.

"Why set this boat adrift?" he reasoned. "It is too good a boat to treat that way, and, besides, it will make a good place for me to spend the rest of the night. I've got to stay around here until morning, and then I'll see if I can't get help. I'll just appropriate this boat for my own use They have dad's model, and I'll take their boat."

Softly he got into the craft, and with an oar which was kept in it to propel it in case the engine gave out, he poled it along the shore of the lake until he was some distance away from the dock.

That afternoon he had seen a secluded place along the shore, a spot where overhanging bushes made a good hiding place, and for this he headed the craft. A little later it was completely out of sight, and Tom stretched out on the cushioned seats, pulling a tarpaulin over him. There he prepared to spend the rest of the night.

"They can't get away except through the woods now, which I don't believe they'll do," he thought, "and this is better for me than staying out under a tree. I'm glad I thought of it."

The youth, naturally, did not pass a very comfortable night, though his bed was not a half bad one. He fell into uneasy dozes, only to arouse, thinking the men in the old mansion were trying to escape. Then he would sit up and listen, but he could hear nothing. It seemed as if morning would never come, but at length the stars began to fade, and the sky seemed overcast with a filmy, white veil. Tom sat up, rubbed his smarting eyes, and stretched his cramped limbs.

"Oh, for a hot cup of coffee!" he exclaimed. "But not for mine, until I land these chaps where they belong. Now the question is, how can I get help to capture them?"

His hunger was forgotten in this. He stepped from the boat to a secluded spot on the shore. The craft, he noted, was well hidden.

"I've got to go back to where I left my motor-cycle, jump on that, and ride for aid," he reasoned. "Maybe I can get the charcoal-burner to go for me, while I come back and stand guard. I guess that would be the best plan. I certainly ought to be on hand, for there is no telling when these fellows will skip out with the model, if they haven't gone already. I hate to leave, yet I've got to. It's the only way. I wish I'd done as dad suggested, and brought help. But it's too late for that. Well, I'm off."

Tom took a last look at the motor-boat, which was a fine one. He wished it was his. Then he struck through the woods. He had his bearings now, and was soon at the place where he had left his machine. It had not been disturbed. He caught a glimpse of the old mansion on his way out of the woods. There appeared to be no one stirring about it.

"I hope my birds haven't flown!" he exclaimed, and the thought gave him such uneasiness that he put it from him. Pushing his heavy machine ahead of him until he came to a good road, he mounted it, and was soon at the charcoal-burner's shack. There came no answer to his knock, and Tom pushed open the door. The old man was not in. Tom could not send him for help.

"My luck seems to be against me!" he murmured. "But I can get something to eat here, anyhow. I'm almost starved!"

He found the kitchen utensils, and made some coffee, also frying some bacon and eggs. Then, feeling much refreshed, and having left on the table some money to pay for the inroad he had made on the victuals, he started to go outside.

As our hero stepped to the door he was greeted by a savage growl that made him start in alarm.

"A dog!" he mused. "I didn't know there was one around."

He looked outside and there, to his dismay, saw a big, savage-appearing bulldog standing close to where he had left his motor-cycle. The animal had been sniffing suspiciously at the machine.

"Good dog!" called Tom. "Come here!"

But the bulldog did not come. Instead the beast stood still, showed his teeth to Tom and growled in a low tone.

"Wonder if the owner can be near?" mused the young inventor. "That dog won't let me get my machine, I am afraid."

Tom spoke to the animal again and again the dog growled and showed his teeth. He next made a move as if to leap into the house, and Tom quickly stepped back and banged shut the door.

"Well, if this isn't the worst yet!" cried the youth to himself. "Here, just at the time I want to be off, I must be held up by such a brute as that outside. Wonder how long he'll keep me a prisoner?"

Tom went to a window and peered out. No person had appeared and the lad rightly surmised that the bulldog had come to the cottage alone. The beast appeared to be hungry, and this gave Tom a sudden idea.

"Maybe if I feed him, he'll forget that I am around and give me a chance to get away," he reasoned. "Guess I had better try that dodge on him."

Tom looked around the cottage and at last found the remains of a chicken dinner the owner had left behind. He picked up some of the bones and called the bulldog. The animal came up rather suspiciously. Tom threw him one bone, which he proceeded to crunch up vigorously.

"He's hungry right enough," mused Tom. "I guess he'd like to sample my leg. But he's not going to do it—not if I can help it."

At the back of the cottage was a little shed, the door to which stood open. Tom threw a bone near to the door of this shed and then managed to throw another bone inside the place. The bulldog found the first bone and then disappeared after the second.

"Now is my time, I guess," the young inventor

told himself, and watching his chance, he ran from the cottage toward his motor-cycle. He made no noise and quickly shoved the machine into the roadway. Just as he turned on the power the bulldog came out of the shed, barking furiously.

"You've missed it!" said Tom grimly as the machine started, and quickly the cottage and the bulldog were left behind. The road was rough for a short distance and he had to pay strict attention to what he was doing.

"I've got to ride to the nearest village," he said. "It's a long distance, and, in the meanwhile, the men may escape. But I can't do anything else. I dare not tackle them alone, and there is no telling when the charcoal-burner may come back. I've got to make speed, that's all."

Out on the main road the lad sent his machine ahead at a fast pace. He was fairly humming along when, suddenly, from around a curve in the highway he heard the "honk-honk" of an automobile horn. For an instant his heart failed him.

"I wonder if those are the thieves? Maybe they have left the house, and are in their auto!" he whispered as he slowed down his machine.

The automobile appeared to have halted. As Tom came nearer the turn he heard voices. At the sound of one he started. The voice exclaimed:

"Bless my spectacles! What's wrong now? I thought that when I got this automobile I would enjoy life, but it's as bad as my motor-cycle was for going wrong! Bless my very existence, but has anything happened?"

"Mr. Damon!" exclaimed Tom, for he recognized the eccentric individual of whom he had obtained the motor-cycle.

The next moment Tom was in sight of a big touring car, containing, not only Mr. Damon, whom Tom recognized at once, but three other gentlemen.

"Oh, Mr. Damon," cried Tom, "will you help me capture a gang of thieves? They are in a deserted mansion in the woods, and they have one of my father's patent models! Will you help me, Mr. Damon?"

"Why, bless my top-knot!" exclaimed the odd gentleman. "If it isn't Tom Swift, the young inventor! Bless my very happiness! There's my motor-cycle, too! Help you? Why, of course we will. Bless my shoe-leather! Of course we'll help you!"

CHAPTER XXV

THE CAPTURE—GOOD-BY

Tom's story was soon told, and Mr. Damon quickly explained to his friends in the automobile how he had first made the acquaintance of the young inventor.

"But how does it happen that you are trusting yourself in a car like this?" asked Tom. "I thought you were done with gasolene machines, Mr. Damon."

"I thought so, too, Tom, but, bless my batteries, my doctor insisted that I must get out in the open air. I'm too stout to walk, and I can't run. The only solution was in an automobile, for I never would dream of a motor-cycle. I wonder that one of mine hasn't run away with you and killed you. But there! My automobile is nearly as bad. We went along very nicely yesterday, and now, just when I have a party of friends out, something goes wrong. Bless my liver! I do seem to have the worst luck!"

Tom lost no time in looking for the trouble. He found it in the ignition, and soon had it fixed. Then a sort of council of war was held.

"Do you think those scoundrels are there yet?" asked Mr. Damon.

"I hope so," answered Tom.

"So do I," went on the odd character. "Bless my soul, but I want a chance to pummel them. Come, gentlemen, let's be moving. Will you ride with us, Tom Swift, or on that dangerous motor-cycle?"

"I think I'll stick to my machine, Mr. Damon. I can easily keep up with you."

"Very well. Then we'll get along. We'll proceed until we get close to the old mansion, and then some of us will go down to the lake shore, and the rest of us will surround the house. We'll catch the villains red-handed, and I hope we bag that tramp among them."

"I hardly think he is there," said Tom.

In a short time the auto and the motor-cycle had carried the respective riders to the road through the woods. There the machines were left, and the party proceeded on foot. Tom had a revolver with him, and one member of Mr. Damon's party also had a small one, more to scare dogs than for any other purpose. Tom gave his weapon to one of the men, and cut a stout stick for himself, an example followed by those who had no firearms.

"A club for mine!" exclaimed Mr. Damon. "The less I have to do with machinery the better I like it. Now, Tom Swift is just the other way around," he explained to his friends.

Cautiously they approached the house, and when within seeing distance of it they paused for a consultation. There seemed to be no one stirring about the old mansion, and Tom was fearful lest the men had left. But this could not be determined until they came closer. Two of Mr. Damon's friends elected to go down to the shore of the lake and prevent any escape in that direction, while the others, including Tom, were to approach from the wood side. When the two who were to form the water attacking party were ready, one of them was to fire his revolver as a signal. Then Tom, Mr. Damon and the others would rush in.

The young inventor, Mr. Damon, and his friend, whom he addressed as Mr. Benson, went as close to the house as they considered prudent. Then, screening themselves in the bushes, they waited. They conversed in whispers, Tom giving more details of his experience with the patent thieves.

Suddenly the silence of the woods was broken by some one advancing through the underbrush.

"Bless my gaiters, some one is coming!" exclaimed Mr. Damon in a hoarse whisper. "Can that be Munson or Dwight coming back?" He referred to his two friends who had gone to the lake.

"Or perhaps the fellows are escaping," suggested Mr. Benson. "Suppose we take a look."

At that moment the person approaching, whoever he was, began to sing. Tom started.

"I'll wager that's Happy Harry, the tramp!" he exclaimed. "I know his voice."

Cautiously Tom peered over the screen of bushes.

"Who is it?" asked Mr. Damon.

"It's Happy Harry!" said Tom. "We'll get them all, now. He's going up to the house."

They watched the tramp. All unconscious of the eyes of the men and boy in the bushes, he kept on. Presently the door of the house opened, and a man came out. Tom recognized him as Anson Morse—the person who had dropped the telegram.

"Say, Burke," called the man at the door, "have you taken the motor-boat?"

"Motor-boat? No," answered the tramp. "I just came here. I've had a hard time—nearly got caught in Swift's house the other night by that cub of a boy. Is the boat gone?"

"Yes. Appleson came back in it last night and saw some one looking in the window, but we thought it was only a farmer and chased him away. This morning the boat's gone. I thought maybe you had taken it for a joke."

"Not a bit of it! Something's wrong!" exclaimed Happy Harry. "We'd better light out. I think the police are after us. That young Swift is too sharp for my liking. We'd better skip. I don't believe that was a farmer who looked in the window. Tell the others, get the stuff, and we'll leave this locality."

"They're here still," whispered Tom. "That's good!"

"I wonder if Munson and Dwight are at the lake yet?" asked Mr. Damon. "They ought to be——"

At that instant a pistol shot rang out. The tramp, after a hasty glance around, started on the run for the house. The man in the doorway sprang out. Soon two others joined him.

"Who fired that shot?" cried Morse.

"Come on, Tom!" cried Mr. Damon, grabbing up his club and springing from the bushes. "Our friends have arrived!" The young inventor and Mr. Benson followed him.

No sooner had they come into the open space in front of the house than they were seen. At the same instant, from the rear, in the direction of the lake, came Mr. Munson and Mr. Dwight.

"We're caught!" cried Happy Harry.

He made a dash for the house, just as a man, carrying a box, rushed out.

"There it is! The model and papers are in that box!" cried Tom. "Don't let them get away with it!"

The criminals were taken by surprise. With leveled weapons the attacking party closed in on them. Mr. Damon raised his club threateningly.

"Surrender! Surrender!" he cried. "We have you! Bless my stars, but you're captured! Surrender!"

"It certainly looks so," admitted Anson Morse. "I guess they have us, boys."

The man with the box made a sudden dash toward the woods, but Tom was watching him. In an instant he sprang at him, and landed on the fellow's back. The two went down in a heap, and when Tom arose he had possession of the precious box.

"I have it! I have it!" he cried. "I've got dad's model back!"

The man who had had possession of the box

quickly arose, and, before any one could stop him, darted into the bushes.

"After him! Catch him! Bless my hat-band, stop him!" shouted Mr. Damon.

Instinctively his friends turned to pursue the fugitive, forgetting, for the instant, the other criminals. The men were quick to take advantage of this, and in a moment had disappeared in the dense woods. Nor could any trace be found of the one with whom Tom had struggled.

"Pshaw! They got away from us!" cried Mr. Damon regretfully. "Let's see if we can't catch them. Come on, we'll organize a posse and run them down." He was eager for the chase, but his companions dissuaded him. Tom had what he wanted, and he knew that his father would prefer not to prosecute the men. The lad opened the box, and saw that the model and papers were safe.

"Let those fellows go," advised the young inventor, and Mr. Damon reluctantly agreed to this. "I guess we've seen the last of them," added the youth, but he and Mr. Swift had not, for the criminals made further trouble, which will be told of in the second volume of this series, to be called "Tom Swift and His Motor-Boat; or, The Rivals of Lake Carlopa." In that our hero will be met in adventures even more thrilling than those already related, and Andy Foger, who so nearly ran Tom down in the automobile, will have a part in them.

"Now," said Mr. Damon, after it had been ascertained that no one was injured, and that the box contained all of value that had been stolen, "I suppose you are anxious to get back home, Tom, aren't you? Will you let me take you in my car? Bless my spark plug, but I'd like to have you along in case of another accident!"

The lad politely declined, however, and, with the valuable model and papers safe on his motor-cycle, he started for Shopton. Arriving at the first village after leaving the woods, Tom telephoned the good news to his father, and that afternoon was safely at home, to the delight of Mr. Swift and Mrs Baggert.

The inventor lost no time in fully protecting his invention by patents. As for the unprincipled men who made an effort to secure it, they had so covered up their tracks that there was no way of prosecuting them, nor could any action be held against Smeak & Katch, the unscrupulous lawyers.

"Well," remarked Mr. Swift to Tom, a few nights after the recovery of the model, "your motor-cycle certainly did us good service. Had it not been for it I might never have gotten back my invention."

"Yes, it did come in handy," agreed the young inventor. "There's that motor-boat, too. I wish I had it. I don't believe those fellows will ever come back for it. I turned it over to the county authorities, and they take charge of it for a while. I certainly had some queer adventures since I got this machine from Mr. Damon," concluded Tom. I think my readers will agree with him.

THE END

This Isn't All!

Would you like to know what became of the good friends you have made in this book?

Would you like to read other stories continuing their adventures and experiences, or other books quite as entertaining by the same author?

On the *reverse side* of the wrapper which comes with this book, you will find a wonderful list of stories which you can buy at the same store where you got this book.

Don't throw away the Wrapper

Use it as a handy catalog of the books you want some day to have. But in case you do mislay it, write to the Publishers for a complete catalog.

THE TOM SWIFT SERIES

By VICTOR APPLETON

Uniform Style of Binding. Individual Colored Wrappers.
Every Volume Complete in Itself.

Every boy possesses some form of inventive genius. Tom Swift is a bright, ingenious boy and his inventions and adventures make the most interesting kind of reading.

TOM SWIFT AND HIS MOTOR CYCLE
TOM SWIFT AND HIS MOTOR BOAT
TOM SWIFT AND HIS AIRSHIP
TOM SWIFT AND HIS SUBMARINE BOAT
TOM SWIFT AND HIS WIRELESS MESSAGE
TOM SWIFT AND HIS ELECTRIC RUNABOUT
TOM SWIFT AMONG THE DIAMOND MAKERS
TOM SWIFT IN THE CAVES OF ICE
TOM SWIFT AND HIS SKY RACER
TOM SWIFT AND HIS ELECTRIC RIFLE
TOM SWIFT IN THE CITY OF GOLD
TOM SWIFT AND HIS AIR GLIDER
TOM SWIFT IN CAPTIVITY
TOM SWIFT AND HIS WIZARD CAMERA
TOM SWIFT AND HIS GREAT SEARCHLIGHT
TOM SWIFT AND HIS GIANT CANNON
TOM SWIFT AND HIS PHOTO TELEPHONE
TOM SWIFT AND HIS AERIAL WARSHIP
TOM SWIFT AND HIS BIG TUNNEL
TOM SWIFT IN THE LAND OF WONDERS
TOM SWIFT AND HIS WAR TANK
TOM SWIFT AND HIS AIR SCOUT
TOM SWIFT AND HIS UNDERSEA SEARCH
TOM SWIFT AMONG THE FIRE FIGHTERS
TOM SWIFT AND HIS ELECTRIC LOCOMOTIVE
TOM SWIFT AND HIS FLYING BOAT
TOM SWIFT AND HIS GREAT OIL GUSHER
TOM SWIFT AND HIS CHEST OF SECRETS
TOM SWIFT AND HIS AIRLINE EXPRESS
TOM SWIFT CIRCLING THE GLOBE
TOM SWIFT AND HIS TALKING PICTURES
TOM SWIFT AND HIS HOUSE ON WHEELS
TOM SWIFT AND HIS BIG DIRIGIBLE

GROSSET & DUNLAP, *Publishers*, **NEW YORK**

THE DON STURDY SERIES
By VICTOR APPLETON

**Individual Colored Wrappers and Text Illustrations by
WALTER S. ROGERS
Every Volume Complete in Itself.**

In company with his uncles, one a mighty hunter and the other a noted scientist, Don Sturdy travels far and wide, gaining much useful knowledge and meeting many thrilling adventures.

DON STURDY ON THE DESERT OF MYSTERY;
An engrossing tale of the Sahara Desert, of encounters with wild animals and crafty Arabs.

DON STURDY WITH THE BIG SNAKE HUNTERS;
Don's uncle, the hunter, took an order for some of the biggest snakes to be found in South America—to be delivered alive!

DON STURDY IN THE TOMBS OF GOLD;
A fascinating tale of exploration and adventure in the Valley of Kings in Egypt.

DON STURDY ACROSS THE NORTH POLE;
A great polar blizzard nearly wrecks the airship of the explorers.

DON STURDY IN THE LAND OF VOLCANOES;
An absorbing tale of adventures among the volcanoes of Alaska.

DON STURDY IN THE PORT OF LOST SHIPS;
This story is just full of exciting and fearful experiences on the sea.

DON STURDY AMONG THE GORILLAS;
A thrilling story of adventure in darkest Africa. Don is carried over a mighty waterfall into the heart of gorilla land.

DON STURDY CAPTURED BY HEAD HUNTERS;
Don and his party are wrecked in Borneo and have thrilling adventures among the head hunters.

DON STURDY IN LION LAND;
Don and his uncles organize an expedition to capture some extra large lions alive.

GROSSET & DUNLAP, *Publishers,* NEW YORK

THE RADIO BOYS SERIES

(Trademark Registered)

By ALLEN CHAPMAN

Author of the "Railroad Series," Etc.

**Individual Colored Wrappers. Illustrated.
Every Volume Complete in Itself.**

A new series for boys giving full details of radio work, both in sending and receiving—telling how small and large amateur sets can be made and operated, and how some boys got a lot of fun and adventure out of what they did. Each volume from first to last is so thoroughly fascinating, so strictly up-to-date and accurate, we feel sure all lads will peruse them with great delight.

Each volume has a Foreword by Jack Binns, the well-known radio expert.

THE RADIO BOYS' FIRST WIRELESS
THE RADIO BOYS AT OCEAN POINT
THE RADIO BOYS AT THE SENDING STATION
THE RADIO BOYS AT MOUNTAIN PASS
THE RADIO BOYS TRAILING A VOICE
THE RADIO BOYS WITH THE FOREST RANGERS
THE RADIO BOYS WITH THE ICEBERG PATROL
THE RADIO BOYS WITH THE FLOOD FIGHTERS
THE RADIO BOYS ON SIGNAL ISLAND
THE RADIO BOYS IN GOLD VALLEY
THE RADIO BOYS AIDING THE SNOWBOUND
THE RADIO BOYS ON THE PACIFIC

GROSSET & DUNLAP, *Publishers*, NEW YORK

THE RAILROAD SERIES

By ALLEN CHAPMAN
Author of the "Radio Boys," Etc.

**Uniform Style of Binding. Illustrated.
Every Volume Complete in Itself.**

In this line of books there is revealed the whole workings of a great American railroad system. There are adventures in abundance—railroad wrecks, dashes through forest fires, the pursuit of a "wildcat" locomotive, the disappearance of a pay car with a large sum of money on board—but there is much more than this—the intense rivalry among railroads and railroad men, the working out of running schedules, the getting through "on time" in spite of all obstacles, and the manipulation of railroad securities by evil men who wish to rule or ruin.

RALPH OF THE ROUND HOUSE; or, Bound to
Become a Railroad Man.

RALPH IN THE SWITCH TOWER; or, Clearing
the Track.

RALPH ON THE ENGINE; or, The Young Fire-
man of the Limited Mail.

RALPH ON THE OVERLAND EXPRESS; or, The
Trials and Triumphs of a Young Engineer.

RALPH, THE TRAIN DISPATCHER; or, The
Mystery of the Pay Car.

RALPH ON THE ARMY TRAIN; or, The Young
Railroader's Most Daring Exploit.

RALPH ON THE MIDNIGHT FLYER; or, The
Wreck at Shadow Valley.

RALPH AND THE MISSING MAIL POUCH; or,
The Stolen Government Bonds.

RALPH ON THE MOUNTAIN DIVISION; or,
Fighting Both Flames and Flood.

RALPH AND THE TRAIN WRECKERS; or, The
Secret of the Blue Freight Cars.

GROSSET & DUNLAP, *Publishers,* NEW YORK

THE FAMOUS ROVER BOYS
SERIES

By ARTHUR M. WINFIELD
(EDWARD STRATEMEYER)

Beautiful Wrappers in Full Color

No stories for boys ever published have attained the tremendous popularity of this famous series. Since the publication of the first volume, The Rover Boys at School, some years ago, over three million copies of these books have been sold. They are well written stories dealing with the Rover boys in a great many different kinds of activities and adventures. Each volume holds something of interest to every adventure loving boy.

A complete list of titles is printed on the opposite page.

FAMOUS ROVER BOYS SERIES

BY ARTHUR M. WINFIELD
(Edward Stratemeyer)

OVER THREE MILLION COPIES SOLD OF THIS SERIES.

**Uniform Style of Binding.   Colored Wrappers.
Every Volume Complete in Itself.**

THE ROVER BOYS AT SCHOOL
THE ROVER BOYS ON THE OCEAN
THE ROVER BOYS IN THE JUNGLE
THE ROVER BOYS OUT WEST
THE ROVER BOYS ON THE GREAT LAKES
THE ROVER BOYS IN THE MOUNTAINS
THE ROVER BOYS ON LAND AND SEA
THE ROVER BOYS IN CAMP
THE ROVER BOYS ON THE RIVER
THE ROVER BOYS ON THE PLAINS
THE ROVER BOYS IN SOUTHERN WATERS
THE ROVER BOYS ON THE FARM
THE ROVER BOYS ON TREASURE ISLE
THE ROVER BOYS AT COLLEGE
THE ROVER BOYS DOWN EAST
THE ROVER BOYS IN THE AIR
THE ROVER BOYS IN NEW YORK
THE ROVER BOYS IN ALASKA
THE ROVER BOYS IN BUSINESS
THE ROVER BOYS ON A TOUR
THE ROVER BOYS AT COLBY HALL
THE ROVER BOYS ON SNOWSHOE ISLAND
THE ROVER BOYS UNDER CANVAS
THE ROVER BOYS ON A HUNT
THE ROVER BOYS IN THE LAND OF LUCK
THE ROVER BOYS AT BIG HORN RANCH
THE ROVER BOYS AT BIG BEAR LAKE
THE ROVER BOYS SHIPWRECKED
THE ROVER BOYS ON SUNSET TRAIL
THE ROVER BOYS WINNING A FORTUNE

GROSSET & DUNLAP,   PUBLISHERS,   NEW YORK

WESTERN STORIES FOR BOYS

By JAMES CODY FERRIS

Individual Colored Wrappers and Illustrations by
WALTER S. ROGERS
Each Volume Complete in Itself.

Thrilling tales of the great west, told primarily for boys but which will be read by all who love mystery, rapid action, and adventures in the great open spaces.

The Manly Boys, Roy and Teddy, are the sons of an old ranchman, the owner of many thousands of heads of cattle. The lads know how to ride, how to shoot, and how to take care of themselves under any and all circumstances.

The cowboys of the X Bar X Ranch are real cowboys, on the job when required but full of fun and daring—a bunch any reader will be delighted to know.

THE X BAR X BOYS ON THE RANCH

THE X BAR X BOYS IN THUNDER CANYON

THE X BAR X BOYS ON WHIRLPOOL RIVER

THE X BAR X BOYS ON BIG BISON TRAIL

THE X BAR X BOYS AT THE ROUND-UP

THE X BAR X BOYS AT NUGGET CAMP

THE X BAR X BOYS AT RUSTLER'S GAP

THE X BAR X BOYS AT GRIZZLY PASS

THE X BAR X BOYS LOST IN THE ROCKIES

GROSSET & DUNLAP, Publishers, NEW YORK

Football and Baseball Stories

Durably Bound. Illustrated. Colored Wrappers
Every Volume Complete in Itself.

The Ralph Henry Barbour Books For Boys

In these up-to the minute, spirited genuine stories of boy life there is something which will appeal to every boy with the love of manliness, cleanness and sportsmanship in his heart.

LEFT END EDWARDS
LEFT TACKLE THAYER
LEFT GUARD GILBERT
CENTER RUSH ROWLAND
FULLBACK FOSTER
LEFT HALF HARMON
RIGHT END EMERSON
RIGHT GUARD GRANT
QUARTERBACK BATES
RIGHT TACKLE TODD
RIGHT HALF HOLLINS

The Tod Hale Series

TOD HALE IN CAMP
TOD HALE WITH THE CREW
TOD HALE ON THE SCRUB

The Christy Mathewson Books For Boys

Every boy wants to know how to play ball in the fairest and squarest way. These books about boys and baseball are full of wholesome and manly interest and information.

PITCHER POLLOCK
CATCHER CRAIG
FIRST BASE FAULKNER
SECOND BASE SLOAN
PITCHING IN A PINCH

THIRD BASE THATCHER, By Everett Scott.

GROSSET & DUNLAP, PUBLISHERS, NEW YORK

THE HARDY BOY'S SERIES
By FRANKLIN W. DIXON

**Individual Colored Wrappers and Text Illustrations by
WALTER S. ROGERS
Every Volume Complete in Itself.**

THE HARDY BOYS are sons of a celebrated American detective, and during vacations and their off time from school they help their father by hunting down clues themselves.

THE TOWER TREASURE

A dying criminal confessed that his loot had been secreted "in the tower." It remained for the Hardy Boys to make an astonishing discovery that cleared up the mystery.

THE HOUSE ON THE CLIFF

The house had been vacant and was supposed to be haunted. Mr. Hardy started to investigate—and disappeared! An odd tale, with plenty of excitement.

THE SECRET OF THE OLD MILL

Counterfeit money was in circulation, and the limit was reached when Mrs. Hardy took some from a stranger. A tale full of thrills.

THE MISSING CHUMS

Two of the Hardy Boys' chums take a motor trip down the coast. They disappear and are almost rescued by their friends when all are captured. A thrilling story of adventure.

HUNTING FOR HIDDEN GOLD

Mr. Hardy is injured in tracing some stolen gold. A hunt by the boys leads to an abandoned mine, and there things start to happen. A western story all boys will enjoy.

THE SHORE ROAD MYSTERY

Automobiles were disappearing most mysteriously from the Shore Road. It remained for the Hardy Boys to solve the mystery.

THE SECRET OF THE CAVES

When the boys reached the caves they came unexpectedly upon a queer old hermit.

THE MYSTERY OF CABIN ISLAND

A story of queer adventures on a rockbound island.

GROSSET & DUNLAP, Publishers, NEW YORK

THE TED SCOTT FLYING STORIES
By FRANKLIN W. DIXON

**Individual Colored Wrappers and Text Illustrations by
WALTER S. ROGERS
Each Volume Complete in Itself.**

No subject has so thoroughly caught the imagination of young America as aviation. This series has been inspired by recent daring feats of the air, and is dedicated to Lindberg, Byrd, Chamberlin and other heroes of the skies.

OVER THE OCEAN TO PARIS;
or Ted Scott's daring long distance flight.

RESCUED IN THE CLOUDS;
or, Ted Scott, Hero of the Air.

OVER THE ROCKIES WITH THE AIR MAIL;
or, Ted Scott, Lost in the Wilderness,

FIRST STOP HONOLULU;
or, Ted Scott, over the Pacific.

THE SEARCH FOR THE LOST FLYERS;
or, Ted Scott, Over the West Indies.

SOUTH OF THE RIO GRANDE;
or, Ted Scott, On a Secret Mission.

ACROSS THE PACIFIC;
or, Ted Scott's Hop to Australia.

THE LONE EAGLE OF THE BORDER;
or, Ted Scott and the Diamond Smugglers.

FLYING AGAINST TIME;
or, Breaking the Ocean to Ocean Record.

OVER THE JUNGLE TRAILS;
or, Ted Scott and the Missing Explorers.

LOST AT THE SOUTH POLE;
or; Ted Scott in Blizzard Land.

GROSSET & DUNLAP, *Publishers*, NEW YORK

CAROLYN WELLS BOOKS

THE MARJORIE BOOKS

Marjorie is a happy little girl of twelve, up to mischief, but full of goodness and sincerity. In her and her friends every girl reader will see much of her own love of fun, play and adventure.

MARJORIE'S VACATION
MARJORIE'S BUSY DAYS
MARJORIE'S NEW FRIEND
MARJORIE IN COMMAND
MARJORIE'S MAYTIME
MARJORIE AT SEACOTE

THE TWO LITTLE WOMEN SERIES

Introducing Dorinda Fayre—a pretty blonde, sweet, serious, timid and a little slow, and Dorothy Rose—a sparkling brunette, quick, elf-like, high tempered, full of mischief and always getting into scrapes.

TWO LITTLE WOMEN
TWO LITTLE WOMEN AND TREASURE
HOUSE
TWO LITTLE WOMEN ON A HOLIDAY

THE DICK AND DOLLY BOOKS

Dick and Dolly are brother and sister, and their games, their pranks, their joys and sorrows, are told in a manner which makes the stories "really true" to young readers.

DICK AND DOLLY
DICK AND DOLLY'S ADVENTURES

GROSSET & DUNLAP, PUBLISHERS, NEW YORK